This book is dedicated to
Laurey, who zestfully embraces the certainties
and uncertainties of life, and to
Debbie, my constant inspiration

EMBRACING
UNCERTAINTY

EMBRACING UNCERTAINTY

The Essence of
Leadership

Phillip G. Clampitt and
Robert J. DeKoch

M.E. Sharpe
Armonk, New York
London, England

Copyright © 2001 by M. E. Sharpe, Inc.

Library of Congress Cataloging-in-Publication Data

Clampitt, Phillip G.
  Embracing uncertainty : the essence of leadership / Phillip G. Clampitt, Robert J. DeKoch.
    p. cm.
  Includes bibliographical references and index.
  ISBN 0-7656-0773-5 (cloth : alk. paper)—ISBN 0-7656-0774-3 (pbk. : alk. paper)
    1. Leadership. 2. Uncertainty. 3. Risk management. I. DeKoch, Robert J., 1952– II.
  Title.

HD57.7 .C536 2001   2001020634
658.4′092—dc21   CIP

Printed in the United States of America

The paper used in this publication meets the minimum requirements of
American National Standard for Information Sciences
Permanence of Paper for Printed Library Materials,
ANSI Z 39.48-1984.

BM (c) 10   9   8   7   6   5   4   3   2
BM (p) 10   9   8   7   6   5   4   3   2

CONTENTS

APPENDICES
DEVELOPED BY M. LEE WILLIAMS

LIST OF TABLES AND FIGURES

Tables

Figures

ACKNOWLEDGMENTS

The genesis for this book was a deep and passionate conversation about the way business, political, and academic leaders make decisions. Revelations came as we shared our observations with many colleagues and friends who shared our concerns. They deserve much of the credit, but none of the blame for the insights. A number of students at the University of Wisconsin—Green Bay helped gather data and discuss the research including Alida Al-Saadi, Judy Theil, Dana Goldschmidt, Daniela Ferrio, Lauren Nakonechny, and Tracy Tesch. Professor Tim Meyer, Jeff Bluestein, and Erica Shreck read early drafts of the manuscript and made many excellent suggestions. We also want to thank Paula Wydeven and Dr. Peter Breznay for creating some great illustrations. Esther Clark, Susan Rescigno, and Cheryl Bever deserve credit for keeping this project on the right track. Our colleagues and associates over the years have worked with us in meeting the challenge of uncertainty. Their influence has made us better authors and people.

Lee Williams and Laurey Berk deserve special mention. Lee spearheaded the research effort that provided the theoretical foundation for this manuscript. He was also gracious enough to draft all the appendices. Laurey acted as an unnamed author, working tirelessly, clarifying our sometimes clumsy prose and at other times challenging us to refine our thinking. We could not have completed this book without her. She was with us from the beginning to the end, embracing all the uncertainties of the creative process.

EMBRACING UNCERTAINTY

I feel a responsibility to proclaim . . .
that doubt is not to be feared, but that it is to be welcomed
as the possibility of a new potential for human beings.
If you know that you are not sure,
you have a chance to improve the situation.

—*Richard Feynman* (Nobel Prize-winning Physicist)

INTRODUCTION

Toto, I have a feeling we're not in Kansas anymore.
—*Dorothy*

If Dorothy never heard about the yellow brick road, would she ever have been whisked back to Kansas? Would the tin man have found his heart? The lion his courage? The straw man his brain? The yellow brick road is a powerful metaphor connecting to something deep in the human psyche. It represents hope, direction, and purpose. Yet it also symbolizes a singular promise: follow the yellow brick road, and your dreams will come true.

Transferring these sentiments from a fantasy world to the work-a-day world is as simple as it is troublesome. What if there isn't a yellow brick road, only unexplored territory? What if no one can guarantee that your search will lead to fulfillment? What if you simply don't know if you are headed in the right direction? Most people rarely openly entertain these kinds of questions; privately they experience doubt, confusion, and complexity. The recent graduate publicly professes faith in the career track laid out for her, while privately wondering about the unspoken opportunities. The guru publicly attests to the "seven steps to fulfillment," while privately being haunted by doubts. The manager publicly declares 100 percent support for the latest corporate initiative, while privately harboring unexplored reservations.

The gap between public proclamations and private thoughts is often so great that many people learn to ignore uncertainty altogether. As one employee put it, "Around here, you've got to know all the answers. And even if you don't, you learn to act like you do." In short: certainty prevails, doubt does not.

Our culture tells leaders that they "have got to know." And it tells them in hundreds of ways, both large and small, that uncertainty is bad:

- Interviewers typically expect applicants to adroitly answer queries about career goals for the next five years. If they say, "I am uncertain," what are their chances of getting hired?
- The newspapers are filled with predictions about hot stock tips or the ten best mutual funds for the coming year. How many magazines report on the front page, "Timely Stock Picks Will Not Be Given This Year: We Simply Can't Predict What Will Happen"?
- Citizens often ridicule politicians who don't provide specific plans or promises to deal with every conceivable problem.
- Financial analysts require executives to project next year's earnings down to the last penny. Woe to the company that misses the prediction because of some unknown market force.
- Students frequently insist that their teachers tell them exactly what they will need to know for the next test. Few teachers retort: "I'm not going to tell you because you're going to face many tests in life for which you won't have a clue what the questions will be. You'll just have to hone your intuitive skills."
- Workers often view executives with suspicion when they can't provide the details on market trends, new products, and future investments.

This book takes a decidedly different tactic than the prevailing culture. The core premise is that in many situations, it is in fact better to embrace uncertainty rather than eliminate it. Typically, when people first encounter uncertainty, they try to drive it out with certainty-creating tools (see Chapter 4). Eventually many people learn to tolerate and perhaps cope with uncertainty. Some even learn to accept uncertainty as an inevitable force to overcome. We want to encourage leaders to aspire to something greater—to embrace uncertainty (see Figure I.1). Why? There are two critical reasons:

> *First*, it is important to recognize that there are many things for which leaders don't have answers, they can't make accurate predictions, or they have fuzzy and incomplete notions.

> *Second*, it is important to legitimize "not knowing." Leaders shouldn't feel compelled to provide a definitive answer when one doesn't exist. Unfortunately, there are powerful forces at work in society and organizations exerting a jackhammer-like pressure, pounding into everybody's heads that they have "got to know."

We are *not* embracing a kind of whimsical uncertainty that condones inactivity or a "whatever happens" kind of aimlessness. To be sure, there are many things of which people need to be fairly certain:

- that the sun will rise tomorrow;
- that the airplanes in which they travel will be safe;
- that the computer software will work when they use it;
- that employees will show up to work on time;
- that private conversations will be kept confidential.

However, demanding certainty where none exists is foolhardy, debilitating, and often dangerous. There are many benefits to squarely facing up to the uncertainties of life. In

Figure I.1   **Modes of Managing Uncertainty**

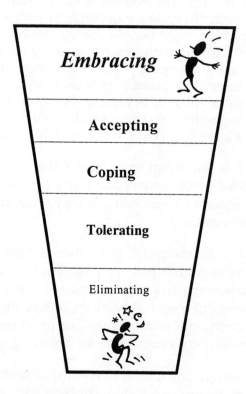

fact, the chaos, complexity, and speed of change in modern organizations require that effective leaders become masters of embracing uncertainty.

Organizations, as well as employees, can choose to either ignore or embrace uncertainty. Examining the relationship between the way employees and organizations manage uncertainty proves revealing. The Uncertainty Management Matrix (see Figure I.2) suggests four basic possibilities about the resulting organization climate:

- Status Quo Climate: Employees and the organization both avoid uncertainty. Employees want few surprises, and they rarely get them.

Figure I.2   **The Uncertainty Management Matrix**

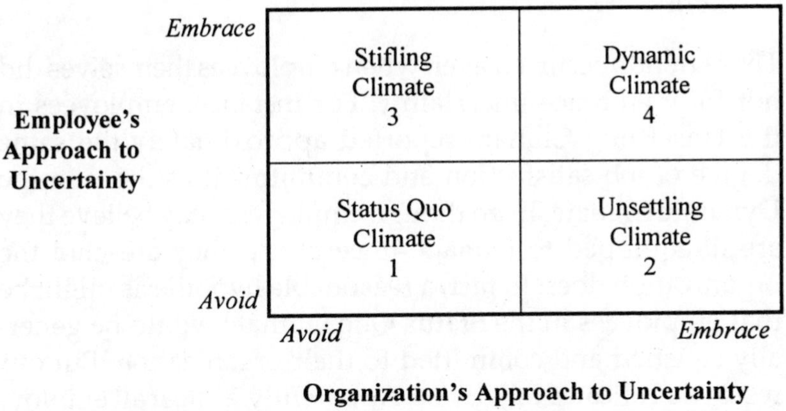

	Avoid	Embrace
Embrace	Stifling Climate 3	Dynamic Climate 4
Avoid	Status Quo Climate 1	Unsettling Climate 2

Employee's Approach to Uncertainty

Organization's Approach to Uncertainty

· Unsettling Climate: Employees desire certainty while they perceive the organization as embracing too much uncertainty. Thus, employees become unsettled and perhaps overwhelmed by the chaotic work environment.
· Stifling Climate: Employees embrace uncertainty, but they perceive that the organization avoids it. The result: Employees feel stifled.
· Dynamic Climate: Both employees and the organization embrace uncertainty. Consequently, the climate is dynamic, energetic, and ever-changing.

By studying over 1,000 employees working in organizations ranging from Fortune 500 companies to small businesses, we developed a tool that allows us to ascertain which climate best described employee experiences (see Appendices A and B or www.imetacomm.com/eu).

The implications are significant. Our research reveals that employees who work for organizations that embrace uncertainty tend to be:

· more satisfied with their jobs;
· more committed to their organizations;
· less cynical about organizational life; and

· more likely to identify with the organization (see Appendix C).

These trends occurred even when employees themselves did not fully embrace uncertainty. For instance, employees in the Unsettling Climate reported approximately the same degree of job satisfaction and commitment as those in the Dynamic Climate. Even though employees may believe they are ill-equipped to manage uncertainty, they are glad the organization does. In fact, a reasonable hypothesis might be that employees in the Status Quo Climate would be generally satisfied and committed to their organization. But our research indicates otherwise. Apparently, almost all employees recognize the need for *someone* to embrace uncertainty.

Employees look to leaders to provide the necessary inspiration, direction, and tools for their colleagues and organizations to embrace uncertainty. We wrote this book to assist leaders in that quest. In particular, we propose the following ideas:

> *Proposition 1:* Embracing uncertainty enhances the quality of life for employees and organizations (Chapter 1).
> *Proposition 2:* There are some powerful forces that make it difficult or socially unacceptable to embrace uncertainty (Chapter 2).
> *Proposition 3:* There is a lot more uncertainty in the world than ever gets acknowledged (Chapter 3).
> *Proposition 4:* People and organizations spend a lot of time creating the appearance, but not the reality, of certainty. This is problematic (Chapter 4).
> *Proposition 5:* The illusions of certainty are pervasive and often debilitating. The problem is getting worse, not better (Chapter 5).
> *Proposition 6:* There are effective ways to embrace uncertainty in your lives and organizations (Chapters 6 to 9).

In the remaining chapters we develop these ideas in a way that enables you to become a more effective leader and chart a new course. Good-bye yellow brick road.

PART I

UNDERSTANDING THE CHALLENGE

1

WHAT ARE THE BENEFITS OF "EMBRACING UNCERTAINTY?"

*It is better to know some of the questions
than all of the answers.
—James Thurber*

- · "Be all that you can be . . . "
- · "Just do it!"
- · "Commit random acts of kindness."
- · "Show me the money!"

Catchy slogans are everywhere. They have a way of grabbing us by condensing a philosophy of life into a few memorable words. "Be all that you can be" is more than a recruiting slogan; it is a philosophy of life that encourages soldiers to face and conquer every challenge. A maxim can become a personal mission statement, shaping your view of life. For example, which person would you rather repair your car: a "whatever happens, happens" guy or a "just-do-it" guy?

The words of wisdom people choose to live by become their yardstick for measuring the quality of their life. They also act as a source of personal motivation. Therefore, leaders need to carefully consider the consequences of adopting the "embrace uncertainty" credo, for it will shape their aspirations, motivations, and accomplishments.

Leaders know this. Consequently, they contemplate the

implications of their credos. As we discussed in the introduction, most employees prefer working in organizations
that embrace uncertainty. But wise leaders want more than
facts. They want to understand the issues behind the numbers. Why does embracing uncertainty increase employee
satisfaction and commitment? Why do employees identify
more with organizations that embrace uncertainty? Why are
employees less cynical in these organizations? This chapter
answers those questions by discussing more specific benefits lurking behind the statistics.

First, Embracing Uncertainty Provides a Hedge Against Overconfidence

Wise leaders clearly distinguish what they know from what
they don't know. This is not as easy as it sounds. The Nobel
Prize-winning physicist Richard Feynman put it best: "The
first principle is that you must not fool yourself and you are
the easiest person to fool."[1] Much of what passes for knowledge is merely a mirage. And frequently people act with a
certainty that only crumbles when the brute force of reality
extracts its inevitable vengeance.

Prior to World War II, the French generals defiantly in-
sisted that the series of fortifications along the northeast bor-
der of France—the infamous Maginot Line—would protect
the country from any Nazi attack. They were terribly mistaken. Perhaps if those in power had been a little less certain, the tragic and almost inexplicable human toll could have
been diminished. Approximately 55 million people were
killed; 25 million were military causalities, and 30 million
were civilian. This does not include the six million Jews who
perished in the Holocaust.

But French generals are not alone. Leaders of any organization can suffer from overconfidence. Success is usually the
culprit. At one time, Sears Roebuck was considered one of
the "best-managed companies in the world" and one of the

nation's most admired organizations.[2] No longer. In fact, some experts believe that the retail arm will eventually wither away. Osborne Computers, Schlitz Brewing, and Schwinn Bicycles, to name a few, have similar histories.[3] In fact, the typical company has half the life span that people do.[4]

Professor Clayton Christensen of Harvard conducted an intriguing and extensive investigation of corporate failure. He concluded:

> There is something about the way decisions get made in successful organizations that sows the seeds of eventual failure... "good" management was the most powerful reason they failed to stay atop their industries. Precisely because these firms listened to their customers... carefully studied market trends and systematically allocated investment capital to innovations that promised the best returns, they lost their positions of leadership.[5]

The "something" lurking behind their decisions is overconfidence in established methodologies, markets, and modes of operation. Of course, companies need to listen to their customers. But not too closely. As Lee Iacocca once said, "no one ever told us to build a minivan." Of course, companies need to watch market trends, but not too carefully because they can obscure new opportunities. Bottom line: The temptation to believe present success equals future success often proves too alluring, even when executives know better. Given this perspective, the philosophy of Andy Grove, the cofounder and chairman of Intel Corporation, that "only the paranoid survive," makes a lot of sense.

Paranoids are mistrustful and suspicious. They embrace doubt. Most people don't. In fact, most people overestimate the accuracy of their judgment. Researchers have developed a way to test for overconfidence (see Table 1.1). People are asked a series of factual questions such as, "How many patents were issued by the U.S. Patent and Trademark Office this year?" Then they are asked to provide a low and a high estimate within which they are 90 percent certain the correct answer will fall (e.g., 3,000–5,000). In one study of over 2,000 people, a whopping 99 percent of them failed this test; almost all were overly confident of their estimates.[6] Apparently, this is a natural human tendency. Of course, "overconfidence isn't all bad!"[7] It is a close relative to positive thinking. Yet overconfidence can lead to unrealistic expectations, overly aggressive goals, and a host of other miscalculations.

If overconfidence is the disease, then feedback is the cure. Only when people test their beliefs, often through trial and error, can they discern the difference between what they *think* they know and what they *really do* know. As two scholars aptly put it: "Experience is inevitable; learning is not. Overconfidence persists in spite of experience because we often fail to learn from experience. In order to learn, we need feedback about the accuracy of our opinions and doubts."[8] Consequently, effective leaders freely acknowledge that there is a lot more they don't know than they do know. But instead of being debilitated by this thought, they can use it as a platform for great achievements. Perhaps the most influential scientist in history, Isaac Newton, made the point most eloquently:

> I do not know what I may appear to the world; but to myself I seem to have been only like a boy, playing on the sea shore, and diverting myself, in now and then finding a smoother pebble or a prettier shell than ordinary, whilst the great ocean of truth lay all undiscovered before me.[9]

Newton's humility stands in stark contrast to the French generals. He is remembered as the quintessential scientist while the Maginot Line became symbolic of how arrogance led to colossal failure.

Second, Embracing Uncertainty Reduces Frustration

Personal anxiety often intensifies when trying to control the uncontrollable, predict the unpredictable, or know the unknowable. Everyone has been in situations where they felt compelled to provide an answer to questions to which they

Table 1.1

Test Your Confidence Level

Answer the following questions by specifying a numerical range in which you are 90 percent confident that the actual answer falls.

	Upper	Lower
1. How many field goals did Michael Jordan attempt during his NBA career?		
2. How many field goals did Jordan make during his NBA career?		
3. How many years elapsed between the births of Sir Isaac Newton and Albert Einstein?		
4. How many words are in the Bible?		
5. How many U.S. soldiers were killed during the Korean War?		
6. What is the escape velocity for a rocket leaving the earth's atmosphere?		
7. How many grams of salt are there in a liter of seawater?		
8. When was Benjamin Franklin born?		
9. How many miles are there from the earth to the moon?		
10. On what date did President Truman hold up a copy of the *Chicago Tribune* and say to a crowd, "Don't believe everything you read in the papers?"		

Source: Adapted from J.E. Russo and P.J. Schoemaker, "Managing Overconfidence," *Sloan Management Review* 33, no. 2 (1992): 7–17.
Note: See p. 26 for answers to this quiz.

didn't know the answers. Perhaps they didn't want to look stupid. Or perhaps they didn't want the boss to discover that they simply did not know. The result: an answer that provides temporary relief, but in the long-term creates frustration, embarrassment, and sometimes regret.

Consider the enormous pressure on law enforcement officials to produce a suspect when there is a serious crime. The victim's family wants answers. The reporters demand answers as they thrust their microphones, recorders, and cameras in front of officials. The public feels insecure and wants action. It's tough to say, "we simply don't know yet." In fact, the pressure can be so intense that any suspect might do. After all, it creates certainty. The reporters go away, the public feels reassured, and the family starts the healing process. Unfortunately, the pressure can be so great that the wrong person is indicted. The public gets its *certainty*, but the officials must live with their doubts. In fact, in recent years several officers of the court were charged with knowingly sending the wrong person to jail.[10] Hopefully, the cases are exceptions, but it demonstrates how difficult it is to resist pressure for certainty.

When leaders learn to embrace uncertainty, they break the cycle of frustration. Consider the situation of a group of physicians simultaneously running their business and practicing medicine. The two worlds couldn't be more different. In the medical world, they have trained for years to detect symptoms, make a proper diagnosis, and prescribe an appropriate treatment. They rarely make tradeoffs, cut corners, or contemplate a marvelous failure. In the business world, they must make decisions based on incomplete data, conflicting demands, and ever-changing regulations. Their frustration emerges from their feeling of absolute competence with medical issues and the seeming futility of managing the business. The physicians naturally try to apply their medical thinking to business "cases" and problems. However, this rarely works. In medicine the symptoms may more clearly point to a particular diagnosis. In business, it may not be so clear; there may be three "diagnoses," or there may be none. During one strategic planning session with a group of urologists, the senior partner had the following insight:

> We can't think of our business like a [medical] consultation. We can make mistakes and no one's going to die as a result. It doesn't mean we are incompetent. In fact, we will kill our practice if we fail to change the way we operate . . . the business, that is.[11]

At the root of the physicians' feeling of business impotence was the mistaken belief that business mistakes equate to incompetence. That's why they delayed making decisions. The senior partner diagnosed the problem, while providing the right antidote for the all the frustration. In fact, this insight marked a major turning point for the business; it not only improved the bottom line, but also improved patient care.

Third, Embracing Uncertainty Fosters Growth, Learning, and Flexibility

Those who are absolutely certain of their place in life are the most resistant to change. Every teacher, coach, and manager has encountered students, players, and employees like these; they are unteachable, uncoachable, and unmanageable. They share a core belief in their infallibility; they know all the answers. And they usually end up frustrated with their level of accomplishment and blame everyone but themselves for their travails. It is unfortunate, because these folks often have some special or latent talent that never gets fully developed. Until they recognize their shortcomings, they will never achieve their full potential.

The oft-quoted maxim "when we stop learning, we stop growing" points in the right direction. But the notion needs to be refined. A particular kind of learning proves most useful. This kind of education requires learners who readily admit their lack of understanding and teachers who know how to foster growth through uncertainty.

Consider the results of some revealing studies conducted by several Harvard University scholars.[12] They investigated teachers who incorporated into their lectures a tolerance for new ideas and a respect for "uncertainty." Students were put in one of two groups: Group 1 was taught a task "traditionally" with an emphasis on the rote learning of steps, while Group 2 was taught the same task with a greater emphasis on general principles and flexibility. The results were revealing. Both groups performed equally well on a direct test involving the task. However, Group 2 performed significantly better when it encountered novel or slightly modified tasks. Group 1 had to rely on a memorized routine or a checklist.

Even subtle changes in language appear to produce this effect. In a similar experiment, one group was instructed with the words, "This *is* a . . ." while another group was introduced to the task with the words, "This *could be* a . . ." Note the tentativeness conveyed to the second group. The results were similar to those in the previous study. Professor of Psychology Ellen Langer summarized her findings:

> The key to teaching this new way is based on an appreciation of both the conditional, or context dependent, nature of the world and the value of uncertainty. Teaching skills and facts in a conditional way sets the stage for doubt and an awareness of how different situations may call for subtle differences in what we bring to them.[13]

Skillful teachers learn to signal "we don't know" by the very language they use. The result: more creative and flexible students.

Effective leaders cultivate their employees in a similar manner, harvesting similar results. Over the past few decades, executives have recognized the need to focus more clearly on customer needs.[14] In the abstract this makes perfect sense, but in practice few companies really do it well. They use the latest tools and techniques: They conduct surveys, talk to customers, and analyze complaints. Yet, somehow, many companies just never seem to truly understand their customers.

The following situation at a dairy plant illustrates this point. The company received several complaints about a particular kind of cheese that did not meet customers' specifications. The plant manager held a meeting with the master cheesemaker about the situation. The cheesemaker responded: "The customers don't know what they're talking about. I make the best cheese in the business." When asked how he could be so sure, he responded: "Over the last twenty years I've been awarded with honors, ribbons, and prizes for my cheese. I'm doing it just like I was taught in school by the great masters." Simply, "he knows; the customer doesn't."

The "we know best" mind-set pervades companies like this. And if company leaders think they know all the answers, the company cannot grow. Like the Group 1 students, they may do well under stable conditions but perform poorly under changing conditions. Indeed, within a year of this incident the dairy plant's market share significantly declined.

Fourth, Embracing Uncertainty Properly Frames Information

A picture frame highlights certain aspects of a photograph, while subtly de-emphasizing others. Information frames work in a similar way, typically accenting the known rather than the unknown. Consider the problem of whether you should carry an umbrella to work. We've all heard of "Murphy's Law of Umbrellas: Despite the weather forecast, by carrying an umbrella to work, you actually decrease the chances that it will rain." The spirit, if not the causal relationship, of this quip is essentially correct. In fact, weather predictions of rain are accurate about 80 percent of the time. That seems pretty impressive. But what the weather prediction doesn't tell you is crucial: It doesn't tell you the precise time and location of the rain. Even if there is a high probability of rain, the likelihood that it will fall while you are outside is much lower. Physicist and computer scientist Robert Matthews explains:

> Probability theory then shows that even an 80 percent accurate forecast of rain is twice as likely to prove wrong as right during your walk—and you'll end up taking an umbrella unnecessarily. The fact is that even today's apparently highly accurate forecasts are still not good enough to predict rare events reliably.[15]

When you acknowledge the imperfections of your information, you properly frame the knowledge gleaned from it.

Unfortunately, few people do so. The space shuttle *Challenger* tragedy provides one unfortunate example. These were some facts on which virtually all observers agreed:

- The predicted temperature at launch time was 26°–29° F.
- The day before the scheduled launch, engineers expressed grave concern over the integrity of the O-rings at these temperatures.
- Initially, the rocket maker, Morton Thiokol, forwarded a "no-launch" recommendation to the National Aeronautics and Space Administration (NASA).
- Under pressure from NASA, Morton Thiokol reversed its recommendation.
- The shuttle was launched on January 28, 1986.
- The seven astronauts died because two rubber O-rings leaked.

Yale professor Edward Tufte believes that the argument the engineers made was "reasonable, relevant, and weak."[16] The crux of the matter was that the engineers had a powerful and correct intuition that cold temperatures were fatal for the O-rings. However, they did not have any direct data to prove it. There was one case in which there was significant damage to the O-rings on the coldest launch at the time. Yet one case can be easily dismissed.

Professor Tufte argues that if the data was charted in the correct way, the devastating effects of the cold could have been discerned. Tufte recommends a chart that visually emphasizes to viewers all that was *not known* about launches at cold temperatures. His approach puts the decision in the context of uncertainty and visually expresses "the stupendous extrapolation beyond all previous experience that must be made in order to launch at 29°."[17] This is something that the engineers' charts and information failed to do. Tufte concludes, ". . . had the correct scatter plot or table been constructed, no one would have dared to risk the *Challenger* in such cold weather."[18] Bottom line: When engineers, meteorologists, executives, and leaders of all types acknowledge the inherent uncertainty of any information and frame their communications accordingly, they increase the probability of proper interpretation and assessment.

Fifth, Embracing Uncertainty Encourages More Thoughtful Decision Making

John Cleese, the wry actor in Monty Python movies and more recently in business training films, enjoys pointing out the difference between two thinking styles.[19] The tortoise style is contemplative and deliberate, while the hare style is faster-paced and reactive. The tortoises have a unique ability to step back and see the big picture. Rather than asking, "What fire should I put out now?" they ponder, "What are the underlying sources of the fires?" They are the ones open to surprises, innovation, and opportunities. And they look for deeper patterns that are the source of enduring success.

Unfortunately, most organizations have a lot more hares than tortoises. So what? The hare latches onto the quick fix. Sometimes this is appropriate, but more often it is not. Frequently, the result is the kind of employee cynicism that has been wonderfully captured in the enormously popular Dilbert cartoons. At the root of employee cynicism is the inability to "accept at face value the official rationale for organizational decisions."[20] Cynical employees often suspect that decision makers have not clearly thought about the real underlying problems and solutions. Political expediency prevails. How do employees come to this conclusion? Experience. In particular, the experience of not having meaningful opportunities to share in decision making or even being informed about what is happening.[21] In contrast, the tortoise allows time for employees to mull over the issues before making a decision, often challenging conventional wisdom. In short, an organization that devalues contemplation naturally spawns cynicism.

The tortoise and hare are, of course, mere metaphors used to make a point. Everyone uses a mixture of both styles. For instance, two insightful communication researchers concluded that:

> Despite the literal appearance of "I don't know" utterances as uninformed and passive, analysis reveals them to involve proactive displays of interactional conduct.[22]

Translation: When you say, "I don't know," others will not necessarily hear "I'm stupid" or "I'm ignorant." Instead, by admitting your uncertainty, you can inhibit hasty decision making and thus encourage further inquiry or deliberation. Interestingly, speakers may not even be aware that this conversational ploy allows them to use a tortoise thinking style. The key is to have a proper balance between tortoise and hare styles of thinking.

Sixth, Embracing Uncertainty Helps Foster Synergy

For decades, textbooks have taught that planning, organizing, staffing, leading, and controlling were the essential managerial skills. Lurking in the shadows behind these notions is the hidden assumption that managers know more than employees. In some cases, this could be true, but that traditional idea is becoming less and less operative. Today, few managers can be effective without a healthy respect for their lack of knowledge. In all likelihood, managers will know less about many organizational practices than those they manage. In fact, managers in this situation who act like they know usually have a debilitating impact on the organization. Why? Because employee contributions will be limited by the scope of the manager's vision. Employees believe that their ideas will be marginalized, so why offer any?

In contrast, managers who recognize the limits of their knowledge are more apt to create synergy. Why? The dreams of many employees are fused into one. Under the old management style, the dreams of one are driven into many. Thus, managers' skills in our age are more akin to *framing* challenges, *influencing* problem solving, and *inspiring* commitment to team goals.[23] For instance, instead of using the planning process to delegate individual roles to accomplish a task, the manager could frame the general challenge and allow the group to parse up the task. Then the manager would seek to influence or guide the team's thinking about their task.

Seventh, Embracing Uncertainty Encourages Innovation

The unknown can be a source of motivation. Jacques-Yves Cousteau could never have plunged into the depths of strange waters without a love of the mysterious. Sir Edmund Hillary could never have scaled Mount Everest without a willingness to face the unknown dangers of high altitude climbing. But it is not only in exploration of the heights and depths of our world that people need to make peace with their ignorance. Almost every important intellectual accomplishment starts with a willingness to embrace naiveté. David McCullough, the Pulitzer Prize-winning biographer of President Harry Truman, may have said it most eloquently:

> I feel that each project I've undertaken has been a huge adventure, a lesson in a world, a subject, a territory I knew nothing about. People will sometimes say to me, "Well what's your theme?" as I start on the new book. "I haven't the faintest idea. That's one of the reasons I'm writing the book." "Well, you don't know much about that subject." "That's exactly right. I don't know anything about the subject—or very little." "And, again, that's exactly why I'm writing the book." I think if I knew all about it, and I knew exactly what I was going to say, I probably wouldn't want to write the book because there would be no search, there would be no exploration of the country I've never been to—that's the way one should feel.[24]

In short, conquering any new geographical or intellectual territory begins by squarely facing our lack of knowledge.

Just as world-class authors and explorers find the unknown exciting, so do innovative leaders. For instance, the design company IDEO has a legendary reputation for developing innovative products. They have worked in over forty different industries designing thousands of products ranging from sunglasses to Palm Pilots.[25] IDEO products routinely win international design awards for creating both functional and elegant solutions to knotty problems. The secret to their success: passionate curiosity, being open to new ideas, lack of arrogance, and commitment to collaboration.[26] As one engineer explained: "At the first hint I don't know something, I ask, 'Does anyone know about this?' If you don't ask for help here, you're incompetent—you're useless to us."[27]

These fervent words reflect a deep commitment to a powerful rule of thumb: Admitting you don't know something fosters innovative solutions. Conversely, hiding your uncertainty stifles novel solutions to complex problems.

Closing Thoughts

A useful maxim seizes people's attention, inspires them, and compels them to action. We hope "embrace uncertainty" does even more. It should engage your mind as well as your spirit. Facts and arguments provide the foundation for our adage. We have presented compelling statistical evidence indicating that organizations that embrace uncertainty build better workplaces. Leaders of these organizations fight overconfidence, reduce employee frustrations, foster growth, properly frame information, encourage thoughtful decision making, create synergy, and cultivate innovation. No wonder employees respond so favorably. Clearly the benefits of embracing uncertainty outweigh the risks. Right? Actually, some people disagree. Their beliefs and organizations teach them to value the illusion of certainty. If leaders truly want to embrace uncertainty, they must first understand the lure and charms of certainty. We now turn to that issue.

Notes

1. R. Feynman, *"Surely You're Joking, Mr. Feynman!"* (New York: W.W. Norton, 1985), p. 343.

2. C.M. Christensen, *The Innovator's Dilemma* (Boston, MA: Harvard Business School Press, 1997).

3. R. Sobel, *When Giants Stumble* (Paramus, NJ: Prentice Hall Press, 1999).

4. R. Stacey, *Managing the Unknowable* (San Francisco: Jossey-Bass, 1992), p. 9.

5. C.M. Christensen, *The Innovator's Dilemma,* p. xii.

6. J.E. Russo and P.J. Schoemaker, "Managing Overconfidence," *Sloan Management Review* 33, no. 2 (1992): 7–17.

7. Ibid., 16.

8. Ibid., 10.

9. Cited by M. White, *Isaac Newton* (Reading, MA: Addison-Wesley, 1997), p. 343.

10. D. Terry, "7 Chicago Officers Indicted in Extortion Scheme," *New York Times*, 21 February 1996, 12.

11. B. Usow, interview with P. Clampitt, 7 October 2000.

12. E. Langer, *The Power of Mindful Learning* (Reading, MA: Addison-Wesley, 1997).

13. Ibid., pp. 15–16.

14. Wise executives also know when to ignore customers' stated needs and look to their unstated needs.

15. R. Matthews, "The Science of Murphy's Law," *Scientific American* 276, no. 4 (1997): 88–91.

16. E.R. Tufte, *Visual Explanations* (Cheshire, CT: Graphics Press, 1997), p. 42.

17. Ibid., p. 45.

18. Ibid., p. 52.

19. A. Fisher, "Test: Can You Laugh at His Advice?" *Fortune*, 6 July 1998, 203–204.

20. J. Dean, P. Brandes, and R. Dharwadkar, "Organizational Cynicism," *Academy of Management* Review 23, no. 2 (1998): 341–352.

21. A. Reichers, J. Wanous, and J. Austin, "Understanding and Managing Cynicism About Organizational Change," *Academy of Management Executive* 11, no. 1 (1997): 48–59.

22. W. Beach and T.R. Metzger, "Claiming Insufficient Knowledge," *Human Communication Research* 23, no. 4 (1997): 562–588.

23. G. Fairhurst and R.A. Sarr, *The Art of Framing: Managing the Language of Leadership* (San Francisco: Jossey-Bass, 1996).

24. David McCullough, interview by Brian Lamb in *Booknotes: America's Finest Authors on Reading, Writing, and the Power of Ideas* (New York: Times Books, 1997), p. 6.

25. "Innovative Design to Improve the Shopping Cart," *ABC Nightline*, 9 February 1999, program no. N990209–01.

26. A. Hargadon and R. I. Sutton, "Building an Innovation Factory," *Harvard Business Review* 78, no. 3 (2000): 157–166.

27. Ibid., 165.

Answers to Confidence Quiz (on p. 15):

1. 21,686.

2. 10,962.

3. 237.

4. The "correct" answer depends on which Bible and translation you use. Assuming you use the King James Version, the answer is 773,692.

5. Because of a clerical error the history books had it wrong until 2000. The Pentagon revised the figure from 54,246 to 36,940.

6. 25,050 mph.

7. 35.

8. In the year 1706.

9. The average is 238,857, but because it is an elliptical orbit, the actual distance varies by 5 percent.

10. November 4, 1948.

Ideally, you only missed one of the quiz questions.

2

WHY DO PEOPLE SUPPRESS UNCERTAINTY?

It's what you learn after *you know it all that counts.*
—*John Wooden*

Superman is the real problem—or at least he symbolizes it. He goes where no man has gone before, fights the bad guys, and saves the world. But he does more than fight evil; he restores order: When the bad guy conspires to reverse the spin of the earth, Superman corrects this minor problem. When the bad guy tries to melt the polar ice caps, Superman refreezes them. But he not only restores order to the universe, he also takes care of the more mundane problems like helping a pregnant woman in labor. What a guy!

Wonder Woman, Batman, Xena the Warrior, and a host of other characters perform similar roles. So does government. Sir Humphrey Appleby, a character in a British political comedy, was not far from the mark when he said, "Government isn't about good and evil, it's only about order and chaos."[1] Likewise, insurance companies sell the certainty that their customers will be able to survive accidents, illness, fires in their home, thefts of their belongings, and just about any other travail. Some companies even sell alien abduction insurance. If you're covered for that, then read no further. There are some risks worth taking. In countless ways society's myths, institutions, and culture tells people that *order is good* and *chaos is bad*.

Consequently, most people expect their leaders to always be right, to know all the answers, and to predict the future with extraordinary precision. Accordingly, many leaders feel duty-bound to behave like Superman or Wonder Woman. For instance, chief executive officers (CEOs) often feel compelled to provide answers even when they are unsure. After all, they are paid a great deal of money to make difficult decisions and provide definitive direction. They may even be perceived as weak or indecisive if they share their doubts. A simple formula captures the expectations employees usually have of their CEOs:

Assumed Job Duties	+	Implicit Social Norms	=	Powerful Certainty Provider

As a result, because many employees assume the CEO will provide the certainty, they may not thoughtfully explore uncertainty, reasoning, "It's not my job." The CEO, on the other hand, may even ignore input from others because his or her job is to provide certainty. The result: a spiral of decision making totally dependent on the CEO's perspective.

Leaders who embrace uncertainty constantly fight these kinds of organizational dynamics. The battle begins by understanding the specific reasons why people strive to drive out complexity, chaos, and doubt in the workplace.

Desire to Control Events

Artificially ridding organizations of uncertainty often creates the *impression*, but not the *reality*, of greater control. We interviewed one manager who refused to talk to his employees about an impending change until he had "all the facts." Even when his employees asked him about rumors, he put them on hold. Meanwhile, the rumor mill worked overtime. When he eventually announced the change, he was astounded by all the "false and misleading rumors" that circulated through the company. The proliferation of communication channels like e-mail and web pages made it relatively easy for employees to access both reliable and unreliable information. He operated under the illusion that he could control the flow of information and how employees interpreted events. Consequently, he lost credibility in the eyes of his employees, as well as an opportunity to build commitment for the endeavor.

The urge to control extends well beyond information management. Almost any management technique taken to an extreme can suppress uncertainty. Those obsessed with time management, for instance, may be able to precisely regulate the meeting agenda while simultaneously losing the opportunities to pursue an innovative line of inquiry. They say, "time simply won't permit it." More precisely, *the way they control the time* will not permit it. Wise leaders know this, allowing deviations from the agenda for some discussion items. They recognize the importance of riding the crest of waves produced by brainstorms. They realize that if you try to control the spontaneous, you will destroy it.

Quest for Efficiency

Companies that embrace uncertainty cultivate dialogue, tolerate mistakes, and spawn learning. These activities all take time away from the "primary" tasks. Frederick Taylor, the founding father of the Scientific Management School of Thought, would not encourage employees to think "outside the box" when there was "one best way." He was fond of conducting time and motion studies resulting in detailed instructions about how to do the task most efficiently. In spite of people questioning his approach, he was a widely sought-after consultant. In theory, he was probably right. For instance, he was able to slash "the cost of boiler maintenance from $62 to just $11."[2] In practice, he ran into all kinds of problems including labor unrest, strikes, and even a congressional investigation.

What did he miss? The human spirit. The quest for effi-

ciency stripped away the sense of worker pride and owner-
ship that comes from learning how to best do a task. In
Taylor's world, no one had uncertainty because the efficiency
experts exposed it, discarded it, and dressed it up in the
"right" clothes. Taylor wanted to clad everyone in his one-
size-fits-all uniform approach to work.

Those days are behind us, right? Wrong. The quest for
Taylor-like efficiency reemerges from time to time. The
reengineering movement in the 1990s is a case in point. It
captured companies' attention by suggesting that they examine existing work processes and redesign them to reduce
costs, improve quality, speed or service.[3] In one case, a manufacturer redesigned the paper coating process, thereby eliminating a job position, saving the company money while
increasing operating speed.[4] Sounds great. Many companies
hopped on the reengineering bandwagon. But the results
were less than anticipated. In fact, in a remarkably candid
book, one of the founders of the movement said: "On the
whole, however, even substantial reengineering payoffs appear to have fallen well short of their potential."[5]

What happened? Reengineering fell short for many of
the reasons that Taylor's approach did. Scientific management and reengineering failed to grapple with the inherent
uncertainty in the workplace and human spirit. But unlike
Taylor, the founders of reengineering recognized the over-
sight. What's the key to making reengineering live up to
the promises? Here's what you need, according to one of
the founders:

- a mind perpetually ready to revolt against its own
  conclusions;
- a mind prepared not for disbelief (nothing so dogmatic)
  but for a constant, graceful skepticism;
- a mind that's open to any possibility, including impos-
  sibility;
- a mind of democratic hospitality to other views (the

present has a *thousand* eyes, not just one); and
· a mind that is profoundly questioning, but buoyantly hopeful.[6]

We couldn't have written a better recipe for embracing uncertainty! Clearly, organizations should strive for efficiency, but they must balance their quest with a yearning for uncertainty.

Preserving the "Peace"

Organizations that embrace uncertainty not only tolerate conflict, they encourage it. But many organizations place too much value on harmony, which often means that employees avoid constructive debate.

One family-owned printing business enjoyed years of success due to their quality service and the charm of the CEO. As the business grew, so did the pressure to add more personnel. At one point the CEO hired his brother in-law, who had the reputation of being financially irresponsible and not being able to "hold down a job."

Mysteriously, not too long after bringing him on board, the company started experiencing financial difficulties. Five years later the company declared bankruptcy. What happened? Shortly after the brother-in-law was hired, several employees privately warned the CEO about the relative's financial dealings. The CEO explained, "I just didn't want to investigate. It would have stirred things up too much. I couldn't believe that he would steal from his own family." But that is exactly what the brother-in-law did. And true to his nature, the CEO never formally charged the family member with embezzlement. The CEO explained, "Things were bad enough, I didn't want to make them worse." Consequently, the CEO preserved the peace and stifled the uncertainty in the situation. But it came at a high cost: losing his business.

Inertia of Success

Too much good news can be a bad thing because it can lull an organization into a false sense of security. Many executives unwittingly operate by the familiar maxim "If it ain't broke, don't fix it."

Continuous improvement efforts typically focus on problem areas while sometimes ignoring new opportunities. For instance, while Microsoft was perfecting their office suite of programs, they came close to missing the opportunities of the Internet. They introduced software exploiting the Internet well after many other companies did. Clearly, the Internet introduced even more uncertainty into a business already fraught with complexity, chaos, and the unknown.

Underdeveloped Leadership Skills

When an organization starts embracing uncertainty, managers often respond with these protestations:

- "How can I lead if I don't know where we're heading?"
- "I thought my job was to tell employees what to do."
- "If I admit I don't know something, then I'll look stupid."

Objections such as these often mask deeper insecurities and originate from a traditional view of management practice. For decades, textbooks have taught that planning, organizing, staffing, leading, and controlling were the essential managerial skills.[7] Using this model, managers who admitted they didn't know "where they were heading" would feel like poor planners.

Management during uncertainty requires a different model and set of skills. Leaders are no longer the primary providers of information, nor the source of all great ideas. Instead, they exert influence by *shaping* the interpretations of information and *guiding* discussions in a useful direction.

Unfortunately, few schools teach these skills. No wonder many people feel insecure and revert back to training designed to create artificial certainty.

Arrogance

On the flip side of insecurity often lies arrogance, which masks doubt, fear, and apprehension. Consequently, some people believe "I'll succeed if I act like I know all the answers." Know-it-all sitcom characters provide a foil for countless comic lines. In days past, it was Barney Fife of the *Andy Griffith Show* or Ted Knight in the *Mary Tyler Moore Show*; more recently, it was Kramer of *Seinfeld*. The comedic brilliance of these actors lies in their close proximity to real-world characters everyone encounters. People who have experienced some success seem particularly prone to suffering from a case of "know-it-allitis."

General Douglas MacArthur was such a person. As Supreme Allied Commander of Forces in the South Pacific during World War II, he conducted a daring campaign that eventually led to the recapture of the Philippines and the defeat of Japan. Then he skillfully engineered the rebuilding of Japan after the end of the war. One biographer described him:

> No more baffling, exasperating soldier ever wore a uniform. Flamboyant, imperious, and apocalyptic, he carried the plumage of a flamingo, could not acknowledge errors, and tried to cover his mistakes with sly, childish tricks. Yet he was also endowed with great personal charm, a will of iron, and a soaring intellect. Unquestionably, he was the most gifted man-at-arms this nation has produced.[8]

Despite his enormous gifts, it was arrogance that forever tarnished his legacy. MacArthur started believing his own press clippings, presuming that his judgments were infallible. They weren't. After upstaging and defying his commander-in-chief, President Harry Truman, he was relieved of command

and the darker side of his character was eventually exposed.

MacArthur's world view stands in stark contrast to Albert Einstein's relativistic universe. Einstein embraced doubt, despite his success and fame. He once observed, "To punish me for my contempt for authority, Fate made me an authority myself."[9] Einstein understood the "virtues of skepticism" and was suspicious of authority.[10] Professionals, experts, and even physicists sometimes abandon this mind-set. They appear to believe, "I'm an expert; I'm supposed to know."

This kind of arrogance represents a fundamental misunderstanding about the nature of expertise. Experts know more than the answers. They know where the frontiers of knowledge exist. They know that the way a person states the problem may unwittingly obscure the actual problem. They know when the answers they give are only approximations waiting for a more enlightened solution. True experts confidently act on their current understanding while boldly embracing doubt and skepticism. Confident? Yes. Arrogant? No. In other words, genuine experts represent the perfect combination of qualities drawn from a quintessential military hero and a Nobel Prize-winning physicist. Stated simply: They know what they don't know.

Unrealistic Expectations

Expectations have a profound impact on how people interpret and respond to events. Just listen to your body the morning after you've crossed several time zones and wake up in a different country. Your body expects rest and nourishment but experiences something entirely different. Thwarted expectations, whether of the physical or psychological variety, often prove debilitating.

Some people, for instance, avoid uncertainty by expecting that more information will clarify matters, reasoning, "I can't move forward until I know everything." Others suppress uncertainty by expecting that experience always translates into expertise, reasoning, "I've invested so much time and money into this matter that I better know what I'm doing." Both expectations prove problematic.

The quest for perfect knowledge always disappoints. Perfection can be the enemy of progress. Henry Ford would never have discovered the benefits of the assembly line if he waited for all the details to be confirmed. Prime Minister Margaret Thatcher could never have waged the Falklands War if she waited for every possible intelligence report.[11] AIDS researchers could never have developed useful drug regimens if they waited to fully understand the disease. Scientists are still not completely sure why aspirin works.[12] Using partial knowledge often creates a platform for even deeper and more profound insight. Generally, the desire for perfect knowledge results in delay and inaction.

The expectation that experience always results in useful expertise presents another kind of problem—overconfidence. After investing significant energy, it's tough psychologically to admit that you may be more confused than when you started out. It seems that there should be a cosmic law that *at least* rewards your persistence. Alas, there is not. The oil companies drill a lot of dry holes before they hit the gusher. But some people refuse to recognize their doubts, acting in confident but careless and misguided ways. They find it difficult to just pull back and admit that they still don't know. In short, their expectations discourage them from embracing uncertainty.

Closing Thoughts

Albert Einstein once wrote, "Man has an intense desire for assured knowledge."[13] In fact, the need to suppress uncertainty may be an inherently human trait. Who could quibble about the importance of becoming more efficient, maintaining control, preserving the peace, respecting tradition, creating personal security, developing confidence, and setting high expectations? Any of these actions *in moderation* can be beneficial. But when there are no counterbalancing forces, people get closure for the sake of closure and answers because they need answers. Essentially, you get certainty for the sake of certainty. And this kind of certainty often has very little relationship to the real forces and trends at work. Perhaps the more important question is, how much uncertainty do you need in life? Before we can answer that question, it is important to have a better understanding of uncertainty. We discuss this issue in the next chapter.

Notes

1. J. Lynn and A. Jay, *The Complete "Yes Minister": Diaries of a Cabinet Minister* (Topsfield, MA: Salem House, 1987), p. 454.

2. A. Gabor, *The Capitalist Philosophers* (New York: Times Books, 2000), p. 19.

3. M. Hammer and J. Champy, *Reengineering the Corporation* (New York: HarperBusiness, 1993).

4. P.G. Clampitt and L.R. Berk, "Strategically Communicating Organisational Change," *Journal of Communication Management* 1, no.1 (1996): 15–29.

5. J. Champy, *Reengineering Management* (New York: HarperBusiness, 1995), p. 3.

6. Ibid., p. 31.

7. R.W. Griffin, *Management* (Boston, MA: Houghton Mifflin, 1993).

8. W. Manchester, *American Caesar* (New York: Dell Publishing, 1978), p. 15.

9. A. Einstein, *Einstein: A Centenary Volume*, ed. A.P. French (Cambridge, MA: Harvard University Press, 1979), p. 124.

10. R.W. Clark, *Einstein: The Life and Times* (New York: Avon Books, 1971), p. 31.

11. M. Thatcher, *The Downing Street Years* (New York: Harper Collins, 1993).

12. C. Mann and M. Plummer, *The Aspirin Wars: Money, Medicine, and 100 Years of Rampant Competition* (New York: Knopf, 1991).

13. A. Einstein, *Ideas and Opinions by Albert Einstein* (New York: Bonanza Books, 1954), p. 22.

3
WHAT IS UNCERTAINTY, ANYWAY?

*Mystery is so challenging as to be intolerable to some analysts,
and so subtle as to be quite invisible to many others.*
—Robert Grudin

We've been talking about uncertainty but have been fairly vague about how we are using the term. What exactly is uncertainty? Of course, it may seem only natural that the notion of uncertainty is kind of fuzzy and ill-defined. Clearly (or is it unclearly?), we don't think the veil of mystery about uncertainty should be entirely lifted, but it is important to clear away a bit of the fog.

In one sense, uncertainty is defined by its opposite. Certainty means that something is fixed or settled. Those who are certain are free of doubt; they are sure of what they know. Most residents of planet Earth are pretty sure about gravity: Every time we jump up, we come down. This is an unerring, predictable and absolute law of nature in our world—gravity is about as certain as it gets.

To embrace uncertainty is to embrace doubt. It is to question what is fixed and settled. Are there places in the universe where people could jump up and never come down? Questions like this suggest an implicit tentativeness about our state of knowledge. Nothing is settled "once and for all"; we hold even our most coveted knowledge as but a rough approximation. Physicist Richard Feynman describes the impact of the theory of relativity in this way:

> The first discovery is, essentially, that even those ideas which have been held for a very long time and which have been very accurately verified might be wrong. It was a shocking discovery, of course, that Newton's laws are wrong, after all those years in which they seemed to be accurate . . . we now have a much more humble point of view of our physical laws—everything can be wrong![1]

This is a remarkable mind-set for anyone, much less a "hard" scientist. Yet this kind of humility toward knowledge is precisely what we are advocating.

What Are the Degrees of Certainty?

We don't believe that you have to make a choice between certainty and uncertainty. There are degrees of uncertainty (see Figure 3.1). This is not an either/or proposition. Thus, a continuum may be the best way to conceptualize uncertainty. Most people could mark a spot on the scale characterizing their level of certainty about the following statements:

- · When I jump up, I will come down.
- · I'm going to be working for the same company next year.
- · On the next flip of the coin, it will land on heads.
- · There are extraterrestrial beings.
- · Elvis is dead.
- · The sun will "rise" tomorrow.

Most of us count on the sun "rising" tomorrow, so it would be on the far end of the certainty continuum (see Figure 3.2). Of course, most people know the sun doesn't really rise at all; it merely appears to do so as a result of the earth's rotation. This is not some semantic trick; it demonstrates how cleverly our language can imbue a certainty that does not exist. And most—but not all—of us would put the "Elvis is

Figure 3.1 **The Uncertainty Continuum**

Certainty	Uncertainty
● Known	● Unknown
● Law-like	● Chaotic
● Sure	● Unsure
● Clear	● Vague
● Predictable	● Random
● Absolute	● Provisional
● Simple	● Complex
● Stable	● Turbulent

dead" statement near the "sun will rise" statement. At the other end of the continuum might be the statement regarding extraterrestrial beings. Many people believe there is a possibility that alien beings exist, while recognizing that no one has conclusively proven it. Even further down the continuum lies the question of whether the coin will land on heads. No one really knows, and there is really no way of finding out until the coin is actually flipped.

Fortunately, we can label some of the points on the continuum: laws, principles, rules of thumb, hunches, intuitions, and unknowns. Identifying these points, as Figure 3.3 shows, can help signal the level of uncertainty.

Laws

There are laws that discourage people from speeding, stealing, and coveting, but these are different than the law of gravity or other "laws of nature." You don't need a lawyer to interpret the natural law. You may need a scientist to explain it to you, but you can't avoid a natural law. In colloquial terms, "You can't fool Mother Nature." Consider the following:

· Law of Gravity: When Shaquille O'Neal jumps in the air, he will eventually come down.

Figure 3.2   **Continuum Examples**

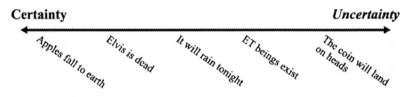

- Law of Supply and Demand: As the demand for Shaquille's time increases, the price of it will go up.
- Law of Probability: Shaquille will miss a jump shot in the next game.

The Holy Grail for scholars is the discovery of these immutable laws that govern everything we do. Yet only a small portion of human knowledge is captured in the form of laws.

Principles

Principles are a little less certain than laws. This is just about as certain as a social scientist can be. For centuries, rhetoricians, speech teachers and, more recently, communication scholars have taught this fundamental principle: *More credible speakers are more persuasive than less credible ones.* This is a fairly rock-solid principle but it is not a law.[2] In almost any field there are some basic principles that guide thinking:

- Personal Finance—Diversify your investments. *Rationale: Risk is minimized by not putting all your eggs in one basket.*
- Management—Involve people in decision making. *Rationale: Those involved in decision making are more likely to support the decision.*
- Organizational Communication—Use redundancy to communicate important messages. *Rationale: Redundancy*

Figure 3.3   **Degrees of Uncertainty**

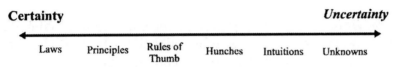

Certainty *Uncertainty*

| Laws | Principles | Rules of Thumb | Hunches | Intuitions | Unknowns |

increases the probability that employees will pay attention to, remember, and act on the message.

Principles tend to be more abstract than laws. They rarely tell us *specifically* what to do.

Rules of Thumb

Rules of thumb tend to be more specific than principles at the cost of being even less certain. Engineers have a rule of thumb that the cost of installing a piece of equipment is roughly equal to the cost of the equipment. Financial planners have a rule of thumb that you should maintain three to six months' of living expenses in a liquid fund. Everyone has rules of thumb that guide their lives. If the paper reports that Elvis is dead, then people generally believe it. As a rule of thumb, the newspaper is correct. But Harry S. Truman found an exception to the rule on November 2, 1948, the day he was elected President. That was the day the *Chicago Tribune* ran the infamous "Dewey Defeats Truman" headline on the front page. The prognosticators and pollsters were wrong, as they were in the Bush–Gore contest.

Most experts have a fairly extensive and complex set of rules of thumb by which they operate. In fact, we could make a reasonably strong argument that expertise actually consists of an elaborate network of rules of thumb. Experts violate their rules of thumb from time to time but rarely violate their principles. There are many exceptions to a given rule of thumb that are covered by yet other rules of thumb. Thus, there is some uncertainty associated with any *single* rule of thumb.

Hunches

The word *hunch* originated from the superstition that good luck was in store for those who touched the back of a hunchback. Good luck enables us to overcome chance by betting on our premonitions and suspicions. Often hunches are based on some sort of unarticulated intuitions. Therefore, an individual can state the hunch while not being able to explain where it even came from, as in, "I'll bet it is going to rain tomorrow."

Intuitions

Intuitions differ from hunches in that people often only have the vaguest sense of their essence. They struggle mightily to even articulate them. The imminent psychiatrist Carl Jung believed that intuition "does not denote something contrary to reason but something outside the province of reason."[3]

In one case, an astute CEO met with his executive team about a proposed new business venture. No one on the team voiced any concerns or could think of a downside. Yet, the CEO was uncomfortable with the tone of the meeting. The wise CEO said, "Since no one can think of any reason why we should *not* accept this proposal, we need to table the discussion until next week." A week later, the team found a fatal flaw in the plan.

A fascinating scientific study provides further evidence of people's intuitive powers.[4] The study involved two groups of subjects: one group comprised of people with brain damage that impaired their decision-making abilities, and the other group of normal, functioning adults. The subjects were given the simple task of selecting cards from one of four decks that would maximize payoffs. But the subjects did not know that two of the decks were rigged to give higher payoffs than the other two. The brain-damaged patients were slow to figure out that the decks were "stacked" and continued to randomly choose from all four decks. The normal subjects soon distinguished the risky deck from the less risky one. Intriguingly, the researchers found that the normal subjects made the "right" choices long before they could articulate their actual intuition.

Even though the study involved relatively few subjects, it provided some compelling hints about the power of intuition. Apparently, people often have the ability to make the right choices, even when they cannot verbalize their rationale.[5] Generally, intuitions are most reliable in an individual's area of expertise. A note of caution, however: A compelling series of studies indicated that the average person's intuitive abilities often falter when predicting probabilistic events.[6]

Unknowns

At the far end of the continuum lie the unknowns. These are the kind of things about which individuals simply *can't* or *don't know* (e.g., what will happen on the next coin flip). For example, if you've never experienced a traumatic event such as a hostage situation or a family trauma, you simply don't know how you're going to react. Likewise, U.S. citizens will never know what would have happened if the United States and their allies had not won the Gulf War.

What Makes Us "Certain?"

Thoughtful people use special language to describe their level of certainty. You can hear people mark their certainty level on the continuum with these familiar phrases:

- "I'm not sure, but I think . . ."
- "I'm willing to bet that . . ."
- "The odds are that . . ."
- "Typically, this is what happens . . ."

· "I have a hunch that . . ."
· "My experience has been that . . ."

This raises the intriguing question of how people ascertain their certainty level. This difficult question has been studied for centuries. The general consensus: *People use various methods to judge their level of certainty.* There are five general methods that most people use: authorities, experiences, gut instincts, reasoning, and testing. It is important to understand the benefits and limitations of each approach.

Authorities

One way of achieving certainty is to rely on authorities:

· If a Nobel Prize-winning economist says that the law of supply and demand explains buying behavior, then I'll accept it.
· If my boss says that I'll have a job next year, then I'll believe it.
· If my guru says there is an alien spaceship waiting for us, then I'm packing my bags.

In many cases, accepting an authority's opinion is the only economical way to create a workable level of certainty. Most people are reasonably certain that the next commercial airline they hop on is safe. Why? Not because they've performed their own tests, but because they trust that the Federal Aviation Administration (FAA) has done its job. Yet, everyone knows of instances when authorities led people astray.

Experiences

Experiences are also used to establish certainty levels. For example, a meteorologist does not need to tell Canadians that it will get colder during the winter. Yet experiences are

always limited. If one lived near the equator where temperatures vary by only a few degrees, then experience would yield
a very different lesson. If our equatorial friends were to travel
to Wisconsin in January, they would quickly discern the difference between summer and winter temperatures. Thus, our
interpretations of experience may lead us to different conclusions.

Gut Instincts

Some people become certain because they just know it "in
their gut." A law-like belief may have its roots in this method.
Or, consider the opening words of the Declaration of Independence:

> We hold these truths to be self-evident, that all men are created
> equal, that they are endowed by their Creator with certain un-
> alienable Rights, that among these are Life, Liberty, and the pur-
> suit of Happiness.

There is very little anyone can do to dissuade others from
believing in certainty derived from "self-evident" truths.
There is nothing wrong with that; everyone makes some fundamental assumptions. But there are times when something
is self-evident to one person that is not to another. For years,
racist policies were justified in light of "self-evident" truths.

Reasoning

Reasoning is another way in which people arrive at some
level of certainty. Most murder convictions, for example, are
based on circumstantial evidence. This means that no one
actually witnessed the murder but that the facts of the case
point to the accused. The jury members use the facts and
what they know about life to fit all the pieces together; this
inevitably involves weighing the various arguments. Thus,
through this reasoning process they determine that the sus-

pect is guilty *beyond a reasonable doubt*. Note that the jury is never asked to make a determination with *absolute* certainty. Usually this works. However, reasoning processes can go awry, as many people felt happened in the O.J. Simpson trial.

Testing

Scientific testing is another way in which we arrive at certainty. Everyone uses this method from time to time. What is the fastest way to the local grocery store? Use a stopwatch to test the various routes. This is a simple but effective way to get a conclusive answer. Scientists, of course, use more sophisticated testing procedures. The central feature, though, is *the objective determination of truth: that anyone could verify the answer if they used similar procedures*. Scientists don't believe that the shortest route to the store is straight down Euclid Avenue just because everyone else does. They test and re-test. But experimental results are not static; scientific conclusions are always open to correction and modification. After all, Euclid Avenue may be under repair, which makes Riemann Parkway the fastest route.[7]

Implications

Table 3.1 summarizes these approaches. Generally, the methods at the top of the chart require less effort and thought than those at the bottom. If you rely on an authority, you don't have to think very much about life. Consequently, those who primarily use methods at the top of the chart tend to be the least tolerant of uncertainty; the guru has all the answers. *How* you arrive at certainty has a profound impact on how you will reach consensus. Conflict is inevitable if people use different means to achieve a suitable level of certainty. It is probably senseless to show your friend the stopwatch if his sole source of truth is a local psychic. Of course, few people rely exclusively on one method. People don't test all their beliefs but accept some on faith.

Table 3.1

Methods of Creating Certainty

Method	Benefits	Limitations	Tolerance of uncertainty	Effort level
Gut instincts	Is expedient	Knowledge is limited	Low	Low
	Is low cost	May be difficult to verify notions		
	Is spontaneous	May legitimize prejudice		
Authorities	Is expedient	Is only one viewpoint	Low	Low
	Encourages development of specialized expertise	Authority may feel compelled to "know it all"		
	Frees us from becoming a master of all trades	Authority may venture beyond field of expertise		
Experiences	Is expedient	Experiences may be limited	Average	Average
	Is universal (everyone has them)	Experiences may be misinterpreted		
Reasoning	Is more analytical and thoughtful	Takes time and effort	High	High
	Is not based on prejudice or stereotype	Data may be missing or nonexistent		
		Methods may be flawed		
Testing	Is objective	Takes time and effort	High	High
	Is open to scrutiny	Requires some level of expertise		
	Can be verified by others	Results may be difficult to interpret		
		Methods may be flawed		

What Are the Sources of Uncertainty?

If you are committed to developing an appetite for uncertainty, then you need to understand the major sources of uncertainty.

Ignorance

Absolute Ignorance

One source involves our level of knowledge. There are a lot of things about which people are absolutely ignorant—they don't even know they don't know. In the mid-1800s, the mortality rate for mothers in some European maternity hospitals was around 25–30 percent and the conventional wisdom was that nothing could be done to reduce the rate.[8] In fact, hospital workers were unaware of how they unwittingly spread infections among patients. Dr. Ignaz Philip Semmelweis soon found the source of the problem and ordered workers to disinfect their hands after working with each patient. Once the medical community accepted this critical insight, the mortality rate dropped to around 1 percent.[9] In essence, patients were victims of absolute ignorance regarding infection.

In a similar way, we can be reasonably certain that today's experts are also unaware of all of the important issues affecting our health, welfare, and well-being. Therefore, our human community will not progress without continually peeling back the innumerable layers of our ignorance.

Knowledgeable Ignorance

There are also times when people know they don't know. Thus, they are aware of their ignorance. This can (a) spur on further inquiry or (b) lead to a search for things they can never know. In the first case, they are searching for the missing piece of the puzzle. In the second case, there may not even be a piece, and they search in vain. In fact, that is exactly the kind of jigsaw puzzles Steve Richardson designs.[10] His company, Stave Puzzles Inc., crafts the most complex and expensive puzzles in the world. One of his devilish tricks is to leave open spaces in the puzzle where a piece is missing by design. It is important to distinguish between these two types of ignorance. Searching for a fictitious piece is not only fruitless, it also wastes precious resources. An even more vexing problem is how much time it takes to conclude that there is, in fact, no "missing piece." This is one of the reasons it may take even expert puzzle solvers up to two years to complete one of Mr. Richardson's puzzles.

Randomness

Even with vast amounts of knowledge, you may be faced with another dimension of uncertainty—randomness. There are random events beyond your wildest imagination, like the freak lightening bolt that destroys a home. There is little that can be done about that.

There is another type of randomness that lends itself to further scrutiny. Whether the coin you flip lands on heads or tails is completely arbitrary. Even a supercomputer cannot tell you whether the coin will land on heads or tails. You just don't know. But you do know from the laws of probability that over time, approximately 50 percent of the flips will land on heads. Thus, you can have a higher degree of certainty about the big picture than about a specific event.

Complexity

Randomness and ignorance are not the only gremlins lurking in the maze of uncertainty. Complexity produces another trap door. The economy is so complex that it may be incomprehensible.[11] Yet analysts can stand back and look at the big picture. We can make two predictions about the stock market with reasonable certainty: (a) the market will go up, and it will come down, and (b) old models of the stock market will be discredited, and new ones will be invented. Meteorologists have a fairly good handle on the myriad of factors that impact our weather patterns, but the interactions are so complex that accurate predictions a month or even a week away can be extraordinarily difficult.[12] Thus, experts may be able to vaguely understand these complex systems, but it will be very difficult to make many accurate predictions.

Ignorance can be a springboard for innovations, discovery, and those serendipitous experiences that make life meaningful. Randomness may cultivate meaningful change, learning, evolution, and adaptation. Complexity can stimulate growth, novel connections, and intriguingly tangled structures.

What Are Some Specific Examples of Things That Are Uncertain?

Anything cloaked in ignorance, randomness, or complexity will be shrouded in uncertainty. That means that there are a lot of mysteries to be solved. We highlight a few examples in this section.

The Future

No one can accurately predict the future. Even highly acclaimed futurists widely miss the mark. Consider the following predictions that Alvin Toffler made in his 1970 book *Future Shock*: There will be widespread use of disposable paper clothing; there will be extensive use of the oceans for farming and human communities; there will be development of subterranean cities.[13]

In spite of these predictions, Toffler continues to produce best-sellers. To his credit, he was right on the mark with many predictions. Moreover, he freely admits the speculative nature of his task: ". . . every statement about the future ought, by rights be accompanied by a string of qualifiers—ifs, and buts, and on the other hands."[14]

Some prognosticators are not so forthright. One research firm actively courts the media and rewards employees by how many times they are quoted in major newspapers and journals. They train their staff with admonitions like, "rid your speech of qualifying modifiers, which make you sound uncertain; speak in short sentences; and repeat important points several times to make sure the reporter gets them."[15] These are the incantations of a certainty merchant.

Predicting the future is not a matter of intelligence. In 1987, Dr. Ravi Batra, an esteemed professor of economics at Southern Methodist University, wrote a best-selling book entitled *The Great Depression of 1990*. It never happened. He even recommended that people keep one-third of their money tucked away in a safety deposit box and one-third under their mattresses.[16] Those who followed his advice lost a great deal of investment income and gains.

Even decreasing the time frame does not seem to help. In the June 1997 issue of *Wired* magazine, several experts predicted that it was "unlikely" that dentists would use lasers to drill cavities.[17] On the very same day that the issue appeared on the newsstand, the Food and Drug Administration announced approval for the procedure.[18]

New Situations

Almost by definition, a new situation brims with mysteries. Many people feel uneasy meeting a new person, searching for new place to live, or even vacationing in an unfamiliar spot. It is inevitable. Their discomfort comes from not knowing what to expect. Chaperons of youngsters to foreign lands are often amused to discover that, despite wonderful local cuisine, the kids always seem to gravitate toward

McDonald's. Why? McDonald's represents certainty in a sea of uncertainties.

The first day on a new job is also filled with ambiguity.[19] New employees experience various kinds of uncertainty such as:

- · What are my responsibilities?
- · How will I be evaluated?
- · What kinds of relationships will I form with coworkers?

Scholars who study the assimilation of new workers into the workplace have discovered seven distinct tactics of "newcomers."[20] The most direct way to create more certainty is to ask questions of co-workers. There are less direct ways such as observing others or even disguising attempts to gather further information. Therefore, even though no one takes a "Reducing Uncertainty" course, everyone becomes fairly skilled at taking the mystery out of new situations relatively quickly. This may not always be beneficial, however, as our stereotypes and clandestine information-gathering activities may trick us into premature evaluations.

Complex Systems

Anything with many parts and many potential interactions between those parts will be fraught with uncertainty. A computer glitch is the inevitable by-product of the various software and hardware system arrangements. All the potential conflicts could never be fully tested.[21] Even a program touted as the most widely tested in history, Windows 95, experienced glitches. As two experts put it, "For complex software, the unpalatable truth seems to be that there are severe limitations to the confidence one can place in a program."[22]

Ecosystems are even more complex. Predicting the ripple effect of introducing a nonindigenous fish species into a lake proves extraordinarily difficult. There is no simple way to make accurate predictions. A system like this may be deemed "computationally irreducible," which means, "there is no faster way of finding out what such a process is going to do than just turn it on and watch it unfold. In short, the system itself is its own fastest computer."[23] It may be of little comfort, but sometimes the only logical choice is to "wait and see what happens."

Human Behavior

Driving a motorcycle through the streets of Los Angeles at 120 mph is foolish. But someone did it. Robbing a convenience store while wearing a work shirt emblazoned with your name and company logo is inane. But a thief did it. Suing the dairy industry for an "addiction" because you chose to drink milk every day of your life is ridiculous. But one litigant did it. Trying to beat a train across a guarded crossing is careless. Yet every year people die attempting to do so.

There are virtually no limits to human foolishness. In one sense, this fact is a source of humor and innovation; in another, it is troublesome. What level of liability should a company have when people use their products in foolish ways? Since it is impossible to fathom the reaches of human behavior, a company cannot hope to predict all the possible misuses of its products or services. This is a fact that the legal system has yet to clearly address. This is why, for instance, a cup of coffee bears a warning label that says "HOT."

Human Knowledge

All knowledge is imperfect because the tools used to gather and evaluate it are limited. Physicist Werner Heisenberg discovered this "indeterminacy or uncertainty principle" as he investigated the inner workings of the atom. He concluded that "the more precisely we determine the position of an electron, the more imprecise is the determination of velocity in this instant, and vice versa."[24] There is a boundary of precision that humans can never cross. This was a revolutionary thought. As Heisenberg's biographer put it, "we can never know nature as it really is; we can know it only as it appears to us as we become part of the experiment itself."[25] The implications of the uncertainty principle are far-reaching. For instance, accurately predicting specific events is impossible. Physicists cannot exactly foretell the flight of a specific electron. But they can predict a range of possibilities. Likewise, you cannot be absolutely sure that flicking on the light switch will result in an illuminated room. There is, however, a 99 percent probability that it will. An insurance company cannot identify which specific individuals in a community will become victims of an accident. But it can predict the accident rate in a given community within a few percentage points. Probabilities, therefore, can be used to create more certainty about the big picture, while providing us little information about a given specific event. In short, you can have greater certainty on the macro-level than you can ever hope for on a micro-level.

Some scholars use the uncertainty principle to argue that the very act of observing something can change it.[26] Consider the impact of cameras in a courtroom. Opening judicial proceedings to television audiences changes the atmosphere in some indefinable way. Likewise, journalist Jon Krakauer reported how his very presence on the fateful ascent of Mount Everest may have compounded the stress and pressure on the team. Would events have been different had he not been there recording his fellow sojourners' "words and deeds in order to share their foibles with a potentially unsympathetic public"?[27] Would the expedition leader, Rob Hall, have pushed so hard without a reporter's pen poised to record every misstep? Would his teammates who died on the mountain be alive today if he acted differently? These weighty questions are unanswerable. This is what Heisenberg taught us.

In summary, the future, new situations, complex systems, human behavior, and human knowledge are inherently uncertain. Thoughtful people should be wary of those who speak too confidently in these areas and should not become overly concerned when they make mistakes or encounter difficulties when confronting these issues.

What Are the Implications of this View of Uncertainty?

There are several important implications of our perspective on uncertainty. This section introduces some of the notions that are explored in more detail in Chapters 6–9.

First, Accept the Inherent Fluidity of Certainty Levels

The level of uncertainty is constantly changing—increasing or decreasing as events warrant. For over 200 years, Isaac Newton's laws of motion were thought to be absolutely certain. Albert Einstein questioned the Newtonian laws, and now they serve as merely good approximations. Similarly, behavioral psychologist B.F. Skinner proudly proclaimed that he had discovered the underlying laws of human behavior.[28] As with the proverbial rat in the maze, he suggested that rewarded behavior will be repeated. If you punish behavior, it will be avoided. Further experimentation showed that, at best, these simple behaviorist "laws" are but useful rules of thumb.

On the other hand, many intuitions have been moved up the uncertainty continuum. For instance, many prescription medicines started out as home herbal treatments.[29] Over the years scientists have discovered the precise chemicals that are the active agents, thus increasing our confidence in the treatments. Your hunch that a job applicant is dishonest may be later confirmed by a reference check. Intriguingly, the very movement on the certainty continuum actually introduces another level of uncertainty. What is certain today may be uncertain tomorrow and vice versa.

Second, Avoid Polarizing Statements About Your Degree of Certainty

Our fictions are as important as our realities, for they tell us much about what we choose to see. Most people choose certainty over uncertainty, the known over the unknown and order over chaos. As we have argued, people generally view certainty as good and uncertainty as bad. But this kind of polarization can be harmful because the opportunities of uncertainty, chaos, and the unexplored are rarely realized.

There is an alternative. You can index your level of certainty, thereby possibly removing the polarizing connotations. If you say, "I have an intuition that something isn't right here," you are inviting further inquiry. Saying, "I don't know but I have hunch that . . ." encourages discussion of the unknowns surrounding a decision. A personal financial planner who acknowledges that she is using a rule of thumb instead of a "law" implicitly creates dialogue around possible nuances of the client's position. In brief, if certainty and uncertainty are treated as an "either/or" proposition, certainty almost always wins. This is unfortunate and unnecessary.

Third, Respond Appropriately to Different Types of Uncertainty

Uncertainty rooted in *ignorance* may be confronted by further study. What could you do when confronted with a software glitch? You could read up on it. However, you may still run into complications beyond your comprehension, like a gremlin lurking in the code.

Yet uncertainty based in *randomness* could never be resolved with further study. Take the phantom cosmic ray piercing your computer screen; no amount of research could solve this problem.

Complexity requires still another response. One way to understand complexity is to step back from the system and create useful rules of thumb. Or you might try to discern a basic pattern in the chaos. For example, no one truly understands how organizations are transformed—they are too complex. However, we know that employees have relatively predictable reactions to organizational change. Employee reactions tend to mirror the stages of those facing a terminal illness; they experience denial, anger, bargaining, depression, and acceptance.[30] Therefore, discerning the type of uncertainty is crucial in planning a response.

Fourth, Recognize That What Is Fairly Certain to One Person Could Be Uncertain to Another

There are people who believe with 100 percent certainty that Elvis is alive or that aliens abducted him. It is very difficult to argue with these folks. Why? They have very different ways of determining their beliefs. Their methods are often unconscious and unscrutinized: "I can't tell how I know; I just know." Thus, it is not reasonable to assume that someone attaches the same level of certainty to a fact that you do.

Fifth, Remember That People Often Misrepresent Their Certainty Level

They may do so wittingly or unwittingly but their motivations are in one sense unimportant. Acting with greater certainty than is warranted can be deceiving and short-circuit critical thinking. Generally, those with a scientific bent are more cautious in their assessment of certainty. They are sensitive to the fact that knowledge is always in a state of flux and that very few things are settled once and for all. Unfortunately, that is not a widely shared conviction. One of the fundamental notions of this book is that people generally present their notions as being far more certain than is really warranted.

Concluding Thoughts

Our taste buds are accustomed to certainty. "The Seven Laws of Personal Happiness" is more palatable than "A Few Nondefinitive Inklings that May Make You Smile (No Promises, Though!)." We feed our appetites for certainty in countless ways. "Junk science" [31] may appear enticing, but it ultimately starves our intellect. This and other treats for the mind will be explored in more depth in the next chapter.

Notes

1. R.P. Feynman, *Six Not-So-Easy Pieces: Einstein's Relativity, Symmetry, and Space-time* (Reading, MS: Addison-Wesley, 1997), p. 77.

2. M. Karlins and H. Abelson, *Persuasion: How Opinions and Attitudes Are Changed* (New York: Springer, 1970).

3. Carl Jung as cited by F.E. Vaughan, "Varieties of Intuitive Experience," *Intuition in Organizations*, ed. W. Agor (Newbury Park, CA: Sage, 1989), 40–61.

4. A. Bechara, H. Damasio, D. Tranel, and A.R. Damasio, "Deciding Advantageously Before Knowing the Advantageous Strategy," *Science*, 28 February 1997, 1293–1294.

5. W. Agor, *Intuition in Organizations: Leading and Managing Productively* (Newbury Park, CA: Sage, 1989).

6. A. Tversky and D. Kahneman, "Judgment Under Uncertainty: Heuristics and Biases," *Science* 185 (1974): 1124–1131.

7. Euclid invented plane geometry in which the shortest distance between two points is a straight line. Georg Friedrich Bernhard Riemann was one of the proponents of non-Euclidian geometry in which the shortest distance between two points might be a curved line as on the surface of a sphere.

8. R. Porter, *The Greatest Benefit to Mankind: A Medical History of Humanity* (New York: W.W. Norton, 1997), p. 369.

9. Ibid., p. 370.

10. See www.stave.com.

11. J.K. Glassman, "An Unfathomable Economy," *U.S. News & World Report*, 3 August 1998, 48.

12. J.L. Casti, *Searching for Certainty: What Scientists Can Know About the Future* (New York: William Morrow, 1990).

13. A. Toffler, *Future Shock* (New York: Bantam Books, 1970), p. 5.

14. Ibid.

15. S. Kirsner, "'Please Quote Me On That': How Forrester Research and Jupiter Communications Vie for Ink," *Wired*, September 1997, 96–105.

16. R. Batra, *The Great Depression of 1990* (New York: Simon & Schuster, 1987), p. 154.

17. D. Pescovitz, "The Future of Dentistry," *Wired*, June 1997, 78.

18. R.L. Rundle, "FDA Approves 'Painless' Laser Drill for Teeth," *Wall Street Journal*, 8 May 1997, B1,10.

19. J. Teboul, "Facing and Coping with Uncertainty During Organizational Encounter," *Management Communication Quarterly* 8, no. 2 (1994): 190–224.

20. V.D. Miller and F.M. Jablin, "Information Seeking During Organizational Entry: Influences, Tactics, and a Model of the Process," *Academy of Management Review* 16, no. 1 (1991): 92–120.

21. P.M. Eng, "A Worried Web," *Business Week*, 30 June 1997, 46.

22. B. Littlewood and L. Strigini, "The Risks of Software," *Scientific American* 267, no. 5 (1992): 62–75.

23. J.L. Casti, *Searching for Certainty*, p. 75.

24. D.C. Cassidy, *Uncertainty: The Life and Science of Werner Heisenberg* (New York: W.H. Freeman, 1992), p. 228.

25. Ibid., p. 235.

26. K. Miller, "Nurses at the Edge of Chaos: The Application of 'New Science': Concepts to Organizational Systems," *Management Communication Quarterly* 12, no. 1 (1998): 112–127.

27. J. Krakauer, *Into Thin Air: A Personal Account of the Mt. Everest Disaster* (New York: Villard, 1997), p. 138.

28. D.W. Bjork, *B.F. Skinner: A Life* (New York: American Psychological Association, 1997).

29. R. Porter, *The Greatest Benefit to Mankind: A Medical History of Humanity* (New York: W.W. Norton, 1997).

30. P. Clampitt, *Communicating for Managerial Effectiveness* (Thousand Oaks, CA: Sage, 2001).

31. Junk science refers to research that has the *facade* but not the *substance* of scientific rigor and objectivity. See, for example, C. Crossen, *Tainted Truth: The Voodoo Science: The Road from Foolishness to Fraud* (New York: Oxford University Press, 2000).

4
HOW IS THE ILLUSION OF CERTAINTY CREATED?

The schools and the books make it all seem so cut and dried.
If you do this, you get this. Well, that's wrong.
—*Estée Lauder*

Magicians, sorcerers, and illusionists have fascinated people in every age and culture. People of all classes from kings and queens to the humblest peasant have delighted in their trickery. But what is the source of the enchantment? Why are people so captivated by their wizardry? To be sure, the mysterious holds a certain charm. Yet, the secret may lie in something even more fundamental—the apparent defiance of natural law. In the day-to-day world, bunnies do not suddenly spring from top hats, and beautiful assistants do not levitate in thin air. Certainty merchants have a similar charm; they cleverly make uncertainty disappear. It is, of course, a mere illusion that vanishes upon closer examination. Any good magician has a magic wand and a top hat. These are the tools of the trade. Likewise, the certainty merchants have their tools that they peddle to organizational leaders. That is our focus in this chapter—the array of specific tools and activities that organizations engage in to suppress uncertainty.

Over-Emphasizing Planning Processes

Proper planning clearly benefits organizations. However, few people address the potential dangers of over-planning. The

CEO of Southwest Airlines, Herb Kelleher, is one exception. He explains:

> Reality is chaotic; planning is ordered and logical. The two don't square with one another. . . . The meticulous nit-picking that goes on in most strategic planning processes creates a mental straightjacket that becomes disabling in an industry where things change radically from one day to the next.[1]

In short, the company can become a *victim* of its planning processes.

Traditionally, the management planning process follows a standard, well-defined series of steps. It typically works like this:

Step 1: End point objectives are developed.

Step 2: Gaps between current positions and the objectives are identified.

Step 3: Action plans, timetables, and outcome measures are created to close the gaps and drive toward the desired results.

The process usually works well. But taken to extremes, managers may drive out even more uncertainty by making the plans more specific and detailed. This quest can turn into a single-minded crusade that builds momentum but blinds the organization to opportunities and dangers. Managers may become less open to input from others along the way and blind to new information that might suggest a needed change in direction. Ironically, *the more they attempt to drive out the uncertainty, the more unpredictable the results really are.* Why? Because they systematically avoid information that might alter or change their plans. Andy Grove of Intel Corporation may have put it best: "When Columbus sailed across the Atlantic, he didn't have a business model."[2]

Executives use many tools to create a business model. *Cost-benefit analysis* is one of the most widely utilized and has proven useful in many situations. But it is important to understand the limitations, as well. Cost-benefit analysis forces forecasters to put dollar values on any number of tangible or intangible benefits. For example, a citizen might be asked, "How much would you pay out of your pocket to have more wildlife (e.g., animals) in your neighborhood?" The problem is that such judgments are somewhat superficial, driving out the complex interactions of various factors. After all, the increase in wildlife sounds good, but what if it also increases the number of accidents at the deer crossings that, in turn, increases the auto insurance rates? These are the kinds of ripple effects that cost-benefit analyses have a difficult time handling. As physicist Mitchell Waldrop suggests:

> All too often, the apparent objectivity of cost-benefit analyses is the result of slapping arbitrary numbers on subjective judgments, and then assigning the value of zero to the things that nobody knows how to evaluate.[3]

When numbers become the focus, you lose all feeling for the unpredictability of the analyses.

Uncritically Using Research

A research study can provide insight into a difficult problem, but sloppy studies can deceive. Merely changing the order of the words in a survey question can elicit vastly different responses.[4] Moreover, surveys are often not accurate predictors of actual behavior. For instance, a detailed analysis of 100 marketing studies revealed that consumers are generally not very good at forecasting their own purchasing behaviors.[5] A consumer might tell a researcher that she is going to purchase a car in the next year, but that response often does not correspond to an actual sale. Consumers may not be lying; they may just be responding in socially acceptable ways. A mother is unlikely to tell a female researcher that she spends more on dog food than baby food. But that is exactly what some studies reveal.[6] Skillful researchers can deal with many of these concerns. But less professional researchers can administer surveys and analyze data in such ways as to create a false sense of certainty. The bottom line: If executives want "scientific" research to bolster their claims, then usually it can be produced.[7] Hence, some research can be dismissed as a mere tactic to increase the organization's confidence in something that is essentially uncertain.

An even more subtle and vexing problem confronts those using research to drive out uncertainty. "I don't know" could mean there isn't enough information, but it could also mean, "I'm confused." More information or research does not always help solve a problem of confusion that may be rooted in complexity or randomness. Ironically, more research may foment more confusion. As organizational theorist Karl Weick observed:

> People can always dig up more information, even if they keep throwing it at the wrong problem. It is easier to solve a problem that is labeled a problem of "ignorance" than a problem labeled "confusion." We deal with ignorance by an infusion of more information. Confusion is not so neat. More information, more quantities, only make things worse. Confusion is an issue of quality, something bean-counters are not well equipped to handle.[8]

All too often researchers try to drive out the complexity of a problem by focusing on too few dimensions. Years ago, for instance, researchers tried to understand human intelligence only by measuring the size of a person's head. It was a simple—but foolish—way to study a complex phenomenon. George Cowan of the Sante Fe Institute concluded:

> The usual way debates are conducted now in the social sciences is that each person takes a two-dimensional slice through the problem, and then argues that theirs is the most important slice.[9]

Likewise, computer modeling can be just another sophisticated tool to produce artificial certainty. Computer models are always based on assumptions, many of which are arbitrary. Moreover, there is usually pressure to make the model conform to the prevailing wisdom. Two noted business scholars concluded that "misinforming the public under the guise of forecasts and computer models appears to have taken firm root in the culture of many organizations."[10] According to their research, senior management frequently asks for adjustments in some baseline figures in order to make the projections appear more favorable. Over 60 percent of the forecasters reported that these adjustments decreased the accuracy of their models.[11] Even independent analysts can fall prey to these pressures. One study reported that corporate earnings projections had an error rate of over 65 percent.[12] Even one of the pioneers of mathematically based forecasting, Thomas Naylor, admitted that "there is increasing evidence that the *politics* of model-building may be the single most important factor in determining the success or failure of a particular corporate modeling project."[13]

Over-Emphasizing Formality in Presentations

A formal presentation provides an expedient way to share a lot of information. It can be illuminating, entertaining, and provocative. But a formal presentation often creates an impression of certainty that is actually a mirage. How does this happen? The speaker comes prepared with dozens of neatly constructed slides and precise diagrams outlining a plan or an idea. He proceeds to review each slide in detail in order to fill up the allotted time, allowing only a few minutes for questions. It all looks very neat, precise, and professional. Nothing wrong with that. Or is there? The problem is that serious questions are rarely entertained in this setting. If someone doubts the premise of the first slide, the question is seldom explored. Why? Perhaps out of courtesy, the question may be delayed or even forgotten. Pressure builds to get through the entire speech because that counts as "doing your job." And audiences unwittingly conspire to "help" speakers "do their jobs."

The net result: The presentation almost always focuses on the known or the projected. Listeners rarely hear of the unknowns or the quandaries the speaker faced in formulating the plan. In brief, a superficial certainty is created that tends to shut off further inquiry, screening the audience from other perspectives that may be based on different premises. Monologue stifles dialogue. Perhaps this is why one of the first actions Lou Gerstner took when he became CEO of International Business Machines (IBM) was to ban formal presentations. He said:

> I have never seen foils (slides) like [I have] in this company. There must be a manual that says every foil must have 4 circles, 2 triangles, 16 arrows, and as many of them as possible should be three dimensional—with shading—and at least 4 colors.[14]

Instead, Gerstner required that all the critical ideas and positions be submitted in writing ahead of time. This allowed the discussion to move forward from that point.[15] He, no doubt, recognized that monologue tends to support convention, while dialogue fosters innovation, flexibility, and mental acumen.

Enforcing Inappropriate Deadlines

Deadlines may be necessary, but they also can be arbitrary. This does not mean they are unimportant, only that they are inherently artificial. Thus, a deadline acts as a bridle on uncertainty. Consider these quips:

- "We don't have time to discuss options; we have to make a decision."
- "If we delay any longer, we won't even have the one opportunity we've already identified."

These verbal gibes crack the whip, keeping the discussion on a narrow track. They act as a stinging reminder to focus and "keep on the blinders." But what if you are not involved in a horse race? Can harnessing a freewheeling discussion be harmful? Absolutely. Reining in a discussion slows the creativity of all participants. Options are not explored, and doubts are not expressed. The result: Artificial certainty is created.

In some cases, people use deadlines to subtly seize power and control. For instance, during one departmental meeting, an intense senior staff member presented a plan for a departmental reorganization. Every detail was specified. All the "I's" were dotted and the "T's" crossed. No one else had provided any input into "the plan." When some members wanted to explore other options, he responded, "Look, we have to reach a decision; the VP wants a response yesterday." When others noted that the deadline was flexible, he went ballistic and responded, "We don't have any other options, and every other department has submitted its plan. We have to decide, and here is a viable option." Even direct assurances from the vice president that this was a special situation with a more flexible deadline would not dissuade him. By the end of the meeting, *his* plan became the *department's* plan, and the deadline was the club used to force a premature decision. For most participants it was a good "under-the-circumstances" decision. What few recognized was that the skilled curmudgeon had artificially and unnecessarily manufactured the "circumstances."

Improperly Using Experts

An outside consultant's credibility may create artificial certainty for an organization: "The consultant said we should execute this plan; therefore, we must do it." Most consultants' credibility flows from past successes, experiences, or credentials. The problem is that the consultants' *ethos* rather than their *logic* may be at the crux of their persuasive appeal. Credibility is something that the consultant does not possess but an attribution assigned by those who do the hiring. The consultant may have expertise, but the value of that expertise is based on the *perceptions* of the organization.[16] In a weird twist, the company *buys* the certainty by the very act of assigning high credibility to the consultant. It is a perfectly subtle method of self-deception. Organizations bottle up uncertainty by letting the "expert" do it for them, whether warranted or not. In fact, some consultants are hired for the unstated purpose of putting their stamp of approval on a predetermined method for driving chaos, complexity, or randomness out of the situation.

The internal organizational expert weaves a magic spell in a similar way to the outside consultant. Internal experts often treat certain aspects of the company as their personal fiefdom, and they defend it against invaders. They also want to make all the calls regarding their area of expertise, and any question about their decision is regarded as a personal threat. This creates certainty at the expense of team problem solving, integrated approaches, and synergistic solutions.

Submitting to Authoritarians

Leaders with a highly authoritarian style tend to share a belief in their own infallibility. They manipulate others by providing certainty in the midst of chaos and demand absolute and unquestioning loyalty.

Tales of tirades, verbal humiliations, and firings have been repeated in countless organizations. For instance, one CEO was so sure of his unerring vision that he demanded that the chief financial officer (CFO) abandon the Financial Accounting Standards Board (FASB) standards when reporting financial results. When the CFO protested by stating that these were "government regulations and we have no choice," the CEO responded, "I don't want it that way; just do what I said!" Consequently, the company exposed itself to some stiff financial penalties from the Internal Revenue Service.

In another situation, the same CEO launched an "empowerment" crusade hoping to solicit more employee input. That may sound a bit odd coming from this fellow; dictators like to call all the shots. But he wanted to be like all the other world-class companies, so he proceeded to outline in precise detail how the company was going to empower people. He, of course, drafted the entire plan without input from anyone, and everyone was relentlessly trained and drilled on the crucial elements of the plan. Managers were required to submit empowerment progress reports, and employees were even quizzed on *the* ten steps to empowerment. Did it work? Of course it did. The CEO had survey results manufactured that showed that all employees were committed to his plan. Dictators know the power of fear—only in a weirdly twisted way were employees empowered. He, of course, never sensed the irony of not involving anyone in planning the empowerment campaign. Thus, certainty and a strange consensus emerged out of this silent acquiescence to the CEO.

Applying Inappropriate Labels

Labels reify; they turn the abstract and fluid into something concrete. Reification can help us understand something that is complex, but there is also a downside: Context and nuance are artificially stripped away. Labels have a way of doing this by focusing attention on a singular defining characteristic. Toothpaste is a good example. The label naturally implies that this gooey substance should only be used to clean teeth and that is how most people exclusively use toothpaste. But it can also be used to clean jewelry or silverware and even fill in an occasional hole in the wall. When Heloise developed her hints, she was actually striking a blow against reification. Another case in point involves the "typing" of an individual's personality. Putting people into categories is as easy as it is problematic. For instance, when people are classified as introverts, others put somewhat arbitrary restrictions on their behavior. Introverts are supposed to be thoughtful and reserved and are not supposed to be spontaneous or talkative. Once applied, the label can constrain the natural ebb and flow of the communication. It directs attention away from how the stage of a relationship or the dynamics of a situation can alter behavior. In the right situation, even the most deeply introverted person may speak without thinking. Likewise, the most gregarious extrovert may become circumspect when faced with a compelling relational trauma.

In the calculus of human behavior, personality is only one variable. The personality profile focuses attention on the individual psyche while shifting attention away from the situation. For example, teams can implicitly cooperate and create a relational dynamic in which they subconsciously avoid certain controversial subjects. Our language contains few descriptive words to talk about fuzzy relationships like this. Yet when leaders implicitly comprehend these relationships, they have a far better chance of accurately predicting outcomes than they do by only understanding one side of the equation. In short, to avoid reifying, use verbs in place of nouns. Instead of "he *is* an extrovert," we should say "he *is extroverting* in this particular situation." Then leaders will have a richer and deeper view of human behavior. Perhaps Dag Hammarskjöld, the peculiarly introspective and deeply insightful former Secretary-General of the United Nations, best summed up the danger of inappropriate labeling: "How easy Psychology has made it for us to dismiss the perplexing mystery with a label which assigns it a place in the list of common aberrations."[17]

Over-Relying on Success Recipes

Success recipes have a tendency to obscure critical relationships between issues and hide critical assumptions. They conceal the underlying thought processes that are used to create the success in the first place. Indeed, this is why 3M uses stories as the principal method of communicating vital information to employees.[18] Recipes can provide a false sense of security.

Typically the "proof" that the recipe works comes from people who have completed all the steps and are enjoying success beyond their wildest dreams. Many of these recipes offer some valuable ideas. However, what the recipe makers don't reveal proves significant:

- How many people couldn't understand the steps in the first place?
- How difficult is it to follow the procedures?
- How many people have followed the formula and have not been successful?

To put this in context, consider the difficulty scientists have in duplicating experimental results. The scientific community has a long and proud tradition of providing specific and complete details about an experiment in order that other researchers can verify the findings. When it comes to details about procedures, scientists use the gold standard—yet the remarks of a Nobel Prize-winning chemist are shocking:

> The startling fact is that almost half of the literature on synthetic procedures we attempt to repeat initially fail in one way or another—that is, they cannot be carried out, to give the yield of product claimed, by following only the directions described in the published paper. A reasonably large fraction of these "recipes" can be reproduced after modification or discussions with the initial author. Some, however, cannot be repeated in our hands no matter what we do.[19]

If scientists using the gold standard get the desired results in only 50 percent of the cases, it would be remarkable to think that merchants of success formulas, using far more questionable standards, could provide reasonable odds of fulfilling their claims.

Concluding Thoughts

Leaders, who inappropriately use any of the techniques described above, can simultaneously suppress their own uncertainty (creating an Unsettling Climate), while stifling their employees' uncertainty (creating a Stifling Climate). For example, excessive planning may make managers feel more secure but discourages employees from expressing their concerns and uncertainty. When the inevitable implementation failure occurs, each side blames the other. The managers argue, "if only they had followed the plan, then it would have worked," while employees think, "if only they had listened to our concerns, then we could have made it work." Such destructive cycles of accusation and blame permeate organizations that overlook the value of developing a dynamic climate in which all employees seek to embrace uncertainty.

Yet, effective leaders, like skilled magicians, know how to expose the illusions shrouding the uncertainty. In his era, Ehrich Weiss from Appleton, Wisconsin, was one such magician. His sensational escapes from straightjackets, handcuffs, and prison cells were legendary. One time he was even shackled, locked into a packing crate, and then tossed into the waters off New York City. He emerged in less than a minute. Yet for all his prowess and ability, he never lost sight of the difference between illusion and reality. In fact, he devoted the last years of his life debunking the fraudulent claims of tricksters and "spiritualists." A man of integrity, he fully acknowledged that his magnificent feats could be fully explained by tricks of the trade. Many certainty merchants purvey intellectual "sleight of hands" by making uncertainty disappear, but only a few have the integrity of Ehrich Weiss, also known as Harry Houdini.

Notes

1. K. Freiberg and J. Freiberg, *Nuts! Southwest Airline's Crazy Recipe For Business and Personal Success* (Austin, TX: Bard Press, 1996), pp. 85–86.

2. A. Grove, *Business Week*, 24 February 1997, 6.

3. M.M. Waldrop, *Complexity: The Emerging Science at the Edge of Order and Chaos* (New York: Simon & Schuster, 1992), p. 332.

4. A. Fink, *How to Ask Survey Questions* (Thousand Oaks, CA: Sage, 1995).

5. V. Morwitz, J. Steckel, and L. Stern, "When Do Purchase Intentions Predict Sales?" Working paper, *Marketing Science Institute*, June 1997, 97–112.

6. J. Mach, "The New Market Research," *Inc.*, July 1998, 86–93.

7. C. Crossen, *Tainted Truth: The Manipulation of Fact in America* (New York: Simon & Schuster, 1994).

8. K. Weick, *Sensemaking in Organizations* (Thousand Oaks, CA: Sage, 1995), p. 187.

9. M.M. Waldrop, *Complexity*, p. 342.

10. C.S. Galbraith and G.B. Merrill, "The Politics of Forecasting: Managing the Truth," *California Management Review* 38, no. 2 (1996): 29–45.

11. Ibid., 38.

12. Ibid., 30.

13. T. Naylor, "The Politics of Corporate Model Building," *Planning Review*, January 1975, 3–28.

14. C. Arnst, "An Exclusive Account of Lou Gerstner's First Six Months," *Business Week*, 4 October 1993, 87–94.

15. S. Sherman, "Is He Too Cautious to Save IBM?" *Fortune*, 3 October 1994, 78–90.

16. E. Shapiro, R. Eccles, and T. Soske, "Consulting—Has the Solution Become Part of the Problem?" *Sloan Management Review* 34, no. 4 (1993): 89–95.

17. D. Hammarskjöld, *Markings* (New York: Knopf, 1964), p. 78.

18. G. Shaw, R. Brown, and P. Bromiley, "Strategic Stories: How 3M is Rewriting Business Planning," *Harvard Business Review* 76, no. 3 (1998): 41–54.

19. R. Hoffman, *The Same and Not the Same* (New York: Columbia University Press, 1995), p. 247.

5
WHAT ARE THE DANGERS OF CREATING ARTIFICIAL CERTAINTY?

When top managers describe reality—what they perceive as reality—with an air of certainty and authority, they create an incredible mantle of ineffectiveness, because everyone then looks up to them to solve the problems, to do the thinking.
—*Peter Senge*

When a talented athlete emphatically slams a basketball through the hoop, it almost always brings the fans to their feet. What's so special about a slam dunk? After all, the team gets the same number of points for a layup. Perhaps fans emotionally identify with the athlete in that special moment of power, grace, and triumph. They may savor these moments simply because they represent a deep yearning for how most people would like the world to work: Most want clear goals, and quick, decisive results. Games of all kinds provide this. But the "game" of life doesn't look very much like basketball, football, or baseball. We live in a messy, chaotic, and untidy world. Expectations are constantly evolving. Results are often ambiguous and progress can be slow. In fact, trying to impose the certainty of a sports game on everyday life can be dangerous. It creates deceiving parameters and provides a false sense of security.

In this chapter, we explore in more depth the dangers of creating artificial certainty. So, go ahead, enjoy the slam dunk, but don't go looking for many in life. Life is far more challenging and complex than any basketball game.

The Cycle of Certainty

A beguiling obsession with certainty presents the greatest danger because it sets in motion a never-ending cycle. We call it the Cycle of Certainty[1] (see Figure 5.1 for how it works).

Step 1: The Need for Certainty Is Created

We have already discussed the powerful forces arrayed to create the need for certainty. Many organizational activities, programs, and processes create the expectation of certainty. For most people, the need for certainty becomes an implicit unstated working assumption. Thus, few people ever actually question if certainty is necessary or even possible.

For instance, during the 2000 presidential election many frustrated citizens were looking for the absolutely accurate vote totals that expressed the "will of the people." Those numbers don't exist now, never will exist, and never have existed in previous elections. Why? Because of countless human and machine errors. Some voters marked the wrong spot on the ballot, some machines failed to register votes, and some election officials misread the numbers. This happens in every election. Usually it doesn't make a difference. But it may have in Campaign 2000: The margin of error and the margin of victory were exceedingly close. Much of the frustration, anger, and angst occurred because of the mistaken assumption that absolute certainty existed in previous election vote totals.

Step 2: The Search for a Certainty Provider Begins

This is an easy step. There are plenty of certainty providers available. Consultants, experts, and authoritarian leaders can

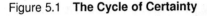

Figure 5.1   **The Cycle of Certainty**

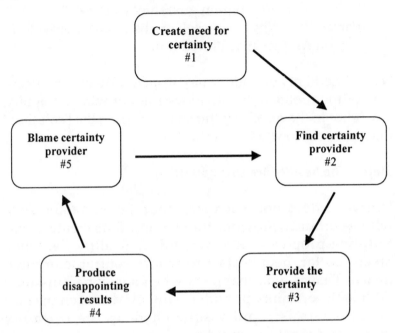

easily bestow the requisite assurances. If you don't want your certainty prepackaged, it can be cooked up quickly using the handy tools discussed in Chapter 4: success recipes, computer models, or cost-benefit analyses.

Step 3: The Certainty Provider Meets the Need

Often the desire for certainty intensifies to such a degree that almost any "answer" will do. The very act of choosing a provider tends to enhance the *perceived* effectiveness of the solution. There are two reasons for this. First, the certainty provider (person or process) is imbued with a high degree of credibility and this makes the certainty provider highly persuasive. But remember the person needing certainty conferred the credibility in the first place. This can create a curious bit of circular logic:

Person A: "The certainty provider assured me that the new program guarantees success."
Person B: "Why do you believe the certainty provider?"
Person A: "Because I hired him."

Second, certainty providers may, in fact, address one dimension of the problem. In situations fraught with ambiguity, any "shot in the dark" will hit something. So the "solution" might appear to work for a short time.

Step 4: The Results Are Disappointing

Everyone does not reach step four. Some people stick with a certainty provider forever and thus create a self-fulfilling prophecy. In a way, this is healthy. Yet when taken too far, people start to ignore contradictory evidence. That is what happens when someone puts total faith in the certainty provider. Any self-doubt on the part of followers is rapidly squelched by the certainty provider's absolute confidence.

Many people, however, eventually realize that the certainty provider missed "something." They may experience other dimensions of the issue that were never addressed. Often their dissatisfaction emerges from a vague sense that "something is still wrong." At other times, it becomes abundantly clear that the certainty provider was dead wrong.

Step 5: The Certainty Provider Is Blamed

Once dissatisfaction sets in, finding a scapegoat proves easy; it's the certainty provider's fault. If people created the illusion, it is simple to cast blame and say the expert was wrong or the consultant wasn't qualified. If the certainty provider was some kind of tool, then the result is the same: "The research was flawed;" "We need a new planning process;" or "We used the wrong recipe."

Step 6: Return to Step Two (Repeat as Often as Necessary)

This is the step when the cycle starts over again—well, almost. The need for certainty remains, so a search for a new certainty provider begins. Real learning could happen at this stage. However, it rarely does. Why? Because *very few people will ask if certainty was really possible in the first place.*

Some Examples

Rumor mills describe this type of cycle. An employee has a desperate need to know something, to have certainty. Someone tells a plausible story that provides certainty. The rumor proves unfounded. But the need for certainty remains, so the employee returns to step two and starts searching for a new story. An enormous amount of organizational resources can be wasted running the rumor mill. The raw material is uncertainty; the finished product is certainty. No one ever seems to think that there might not be any answer in the first place.

Similarly, the *"program of the month"* mentality demonstrates this cycle. Many employees tire of a seemingly endless array of new programs designed to address organizational concerns. They react cynically to each new "program of the month." This aptly named organizational game may indicate that employees are rapidly cycling through the steps described above. The search for the next great answer may be a signal that the last program produced unacceptable results. Then the search commences for the next certainty provider. Inevitably that program "fails" as well, and a new cycle begins. The net effect: No one really expects any new program to address the fundamental issues. Cynicism prevails. Everyone becomes emotionally detached from the new program, which, of course, only hastens the speed of the cycle. Thus, employees learn to silently endure and surreptitiously resist new initiatives because the "program of the month" only gets in the way of doing the real work. The organization never asks if *any* "program" can address the fundamental organizational ills. This is the ultimate misfortune.

You can probably think of other examples of this pattern. It can take years or mere hours to cycle through this process. The critical point: The process itself leads to self-deception, sealing off opportunities to learn and grow. The consequences flow into almost every aspect of our lives and organizations.

How Does the Certainty Cycle Impact People?

Years ago, the psychologist Abraham Maslow proposed that human beings have a hierarchy of needs.[2] Lower-level needs, such as physiological and security needs, must be satisfied before higher-level needs, such as social and self-esteem needs, emerge. At the summit of his model is the need for "self-actualization," beckoning adventurers like the peak of Mount Everest. Mountaineers and others become self-actualized by utilizing their full potential; it's their peak experience or "natural high." But is this really possible with a risk-free mind-set? Can you become self-actualized without embracing uncertainty? We don't think so. But a lot of people still try to do it, and the results are fairly predictable. As Julian Morris of the Institute of Economic Affairs in London said, "If someone had evaluated the risk of fire right after it was invented, they may well have decided to eat their food raw."[3]

Brett was the stereotypical expert. If you had a computer problem, he was the guy you called. He was sharp, competent, quick to make judgments, and very sure of himself. Transferring his natural confidence from his area of expertise to other venues was as simple as toggling between software programs. You wanted a great recipe; Brett knew one. You wanted to know the best place to ski; Brett had been there. He was the expert on everything.

But Brett was also a very unhappy person. He paid a great

price for his artificial certainty. He had few friends and even alienated those when he failed to admit his own mistakes. At work he was regarded as a busybody who no one trusted. For Brett, the two most important letters in the word "team" were "M" and "E." He was engaged in life as long as he played the savior role, but he could never relate to people outside the role; that would have required him to acknowledge others' expertise, and he could never bring himself to do that. Ironically, he frequently lamented that "nobody appreciates me." His self-esteem was so intertwined with his pride and confidence that no one could form the kind of meaningful and appreciative relationship he sought but could not foster; his certainty was the barrier to his self-actualization.

For people lacking ambition, the search for artificial certainty also proves enticing. They want to be told what to do, avoid taking chances, and take comfort in a checklist lifestyle because it limits accountability. These folks present a peculiar managerial challenge. On the one hand, managers like them because generally they do what they are told. On the other hand, they rarely take any initiative and are often resistant to change.

Nancy's tale is typical. She worked in a medical clinic for years and often complained about the mind-numbing routine and nonsensical policies. Yet when management actually sought her input on an impending reorganization, she balked. She demanded to know just what was going to happen. When told that she could actually shape the policies of her department, she wanted nothing to do with it: "Just tell me what you're going to do. And tell me what you want *me* to do." Caught between certainty and uncertainty, she chose certainty every time. She unwittingly lived by Pogo's observation that "the certainty of misery is better than the misery of uncertainty." And then she wondered why she never had a fulfilling career. But like many people, it was in her grasp if she only took a few risks.

Professor of Psychology Mihaly Csikszentmihalyi pointed out that "... many people feel as long as they get decent pay and some security, it does not matter how boring or alienating their job is. Such an attitude, however, amounts to throwing away almost 40 percent of one's waking life."[4] Merely trading time for pay ensures that employees will never become self-actualized. Nancy epitomizes those who fear facing new challenges and living on the edge of their certainty.

Professor Csikszentmihalyi's career has been devoted to the study of "flow," the point at which people face difficult challenges at the cusp of their skills. These are the peak experiences when you become completely focused and hours pass by as if mere moments. As he notes, "... the flow experience acts as a magnet for learning—that is, for developing new levels of challenges and skills. . . . It takes energy to achieve optimal experiences, and all too often we are unable, or unwilling, to put out the initial effort."[5]

Clearly, Nancy was unwilling to put forth this kind of effort. There are few things in life more challenging than learning to face our fears and embrace uncertainty. But that is the way to become self-actualized and experience "flow."

How Does the Certainty Cycle Impact Organizations?

An enterprising economist might find it revealing to calculate the monetary impact of the certainty cycle. Think of all the things you could put into the equation:

Advocating firm positions based on computer projections of limited data.

Broadcasting the latest office rumors.

Consulting "experts" about the one best way to do a task.

Developing detailed planning documents that are never used.

Employing too many people who suppress others' doubts and concerns.

Formalizing procedures that will be quickly outdated.

Gathering more information in the midst of confusing circumstances.

Hiring consultants to confirm predetermined decisions.

Identifying detailed objectives for a plan to be executed in five years.

Justifying decisions that are best made with a flip of the coin.

Keeping up efforts to suppress organizational dissent.

Limiting opportunities by cutting off discussion.

Managing by intimidating employees into conformity.

Nagging employees about trivial details.

Organizing rallies to keep the "program of the month" alive.

Predicting trends with inappropriate precision.

Quantifying every qualitative judgment.

Rationalizing a guru's answer, even if doesn't seem right.

Searching for the perfect plan.

Teaching precise steps in order to master a complex subject.

Using "the plan" as a weapon to force unwise decisions.

Verifying the details of a proposal while ignoring the core problem.

Withholding contradictory evidence.

Xeroxing copies of a fill-in-the-blank mission statement.

Yielding common sense to a certainty provider.

Zeroing in on overly ambitious deadlines.

Billions of dollars are wasted on the pursuit of the certainty phantom, while that time and energy could be spent pursuing other, more important issues. Our superstitions limit our accomplishments; there were no great scientific discoveries during the Salem witch-hunt.

Finding examples from A to Z is easy, but the harder problem is calculating the cumulative impact of these everyday practices. We believe that the fundamental consequence is the creation of the unrealistic expectation that life should be risk free. That has never been the case and never will be. Yet many people hold this expectation and measure their experience by it.

Let's examine the implications of this delusion. Those with a risk free mind-set believe:

- There is always a direct cause for every effect.
- Someone should be able to predict all the possible consequences of an action.
- When something goes awry, there is always someone to blame.
- Ignorance is never a legitimate excuse.

In a risk-free organization, all possible risks need to be identified, cataloged, and classified, which, in turn, can be transformed into rules and regulations. Someone needs to make sure all the rules are followed, so bureaucracies are created to enforce the regulations.

For instance, in the 1990s Mother Teresa was contemplating buying a rundown building in New York City in order to provide care for homeless men. But the onerous task of cutting through unnecessary codes and regulations proved too much for her. The building code required the installation of an elevator, but the nuns who would run the shelter had not only taken a vow of poverty, they also avoided the use of any modern conveniences. They would never use the elevator. Mother Teresa felt the $100,000 extra cost was best spent elsewhere so she abandoned the project. Apparently, even spiritual leaders fall victim to red tape.[6]

Can the Certainty Cycle Be Broken?

Of course it can. But it requires a transformation of employees' mind-sets and organizational processes. Consider what happened at Cemex, a cement maker. For years, the company operated like many businesses: They took orders, processed the requisitions, and sent them to the planning department. They then prepared schedules, dispatched the cement a day later, and hoped the product arrived on time. Sounds like a perfectly logical plan. The only problem was that it rarely worked that way. Drivers got lost, communications broke down, customers routinely cancelled or rescheduled deliveries, and well-laid plans were often in disarray. In short, customers rarely received the cement they wanted when they wanted it. And Cemex employees got an earful of complaints. Nobody was very happy.

What to do? The company could have driven toward greater certainty by refining the planning and scheduling processes. That would have proven difficult with all the vehicles on the road, the traffic delays, and changing weather conditions, not to mention the inevitable bureaucratic snafus. So they tried something radically different with their operation in Guadalajara, Mexico: They embraced uncertainty. They redesigned the entire system based, in part, on how 911 emergencies were handled in Houston, Texas. Instead of planning each day's schedule, they strategically stationed cement trucks around the city, similar to ambulances waiting to be dispatched. When the call came in to Cemex, a dispatcher was empowered to direct the nearest truck to the construction site. In order to do this, significant investments were made in technology. An even more significant investment was made in gaining employee acceptance of the new business model; scheduling and planning practices were radically changed. But there was a huge payoff: fewer customer complaints, less waste and higher morale.[7] Within six months, over 97 percent of the orders were delivered within

10 minutes of the promised time, compared to just 34 percent in another city not using the plan.[8] Cemex even boasted in a marketing campaign, "Now, the concrete is faster than the pizza." One of the leaders of the transformation, Ken Massey, explained the critical insight:

> If I can predict where orders are coming from and can maintain random distribution of trucks, I should always be able to have one close to where it's needed. If I can have a chaotic distribution of vehicles, then I'm really trying not to control chaos, but to use it to my advantage.[9]

Cemex is now testing the model in other cities.

Yet deciding to embrace chaos often proves difficult. Carpenters and tailors are admonished to abide by the aphorism, "measure twice, cut once." Nothing wrong with that—people like their carpenters to be careful. But many organizations go too far. They set up a plan to measure, hire a consultant to tell them what to measure, consult their own experts on the "measuring process," then create a measurement task force, which is followed by an implementation team that needs to check with the consultant about what needs to be measured. Finally, something is cut, and the entire process starts again to determine if the right cut was actually made. We are *not* suggesting that planning and modeling are inappropriate. We are suggesting that companies need to step back from the canvas and ask this critical question: "How much value do the certainty producers really add?"

Employees often take their cues about what is really valued by the company from the implicit structure of their tasks. In companies where planning, accounting, and structuring are the corporate kingpins, certainty becomes a hot commodity. Even if you are not certain, you are supposed to act as though you are. These tendencies create strained relationships among team members and departments. The individuals who "know" are polarized from those perceived as "not knowing" or "not knowing very much." Input becomes superficial, consequently commitments to organizational plans are mere mirages. These dynamics encourage hidden agendas because someone is perceived as "winning" when they "know" and "losing" when they "don't know." No one embraces doubt. No one tolerates ignorance. And it is all counterproductive.

If your organization is rotting from hidden agendas, duplicity, politics, and the like, it is probable that the quest for artificial certainty lies at the core. When a few brave individuals challenge the cycle of certainty, a fresh breeze of integrity and curiosity pervades the organization. Then an invigorating climate of competence and innovation can take hold, just as it did at Cemex.

Closing Thoughts

Scholars Karl Weick and Frances Westley made this peculiar observation: "Organizing and learning are essentially antithetical processes. . . . To learn is to disorganize and increase variety. To organize is to forget and reduce variety."[10]

Perhaps they are a bit harsh. Sometimes we learn something new by organizing in a different way. But they make a point well worth pondering. In the mad rush to organize and perfect, people forget a lot. Neatly ordered mental file cabinets hide complexity and nuance, and the certainty cycle forces them to file away their doubts and intuitions. In the haste to pigeonhole every deviation from the norm, people artificially reduce the natural chaos. The world may *seem* more organized and predictable that way, but there is a price: *You decrease the apparent variety in the world at the expense of reducing your capacity to learn.* You can see the impact everyday. As Mother Teresa discovered, "doing it by the book" becomes more important than exercising sound judgment based on the nuances of a situation. In organizations, more faith is placed on cookie-cutter solutions than on truly understanding the nature of complex problems. On a personal level, many individuals lament the lack of self-actualization while never taking any risks. Certainty at the expense of learning is a terrible price to pay. An education purchased with a little variety and chaos is a pretty good bargain. In the next section of the book, we focus on learning how to embrace uncertainty and create a dynamic organizational climate, like the one at Cemex.

Notes

1. After we developed this concept, we read a book by Ralph Stacey with a remarkably similar observation. His book, *Complexity and Creativity in Organizations* (San Francisco: Berrett-Koehler, 1997) focuses more on the organizational implications of this idea. We heartily recommend it to you.

2. R.W. Griffin, *Management* (Boston, MA: Houghton Mifflin, 1993).

3. Julian Morris, as cited in D. Appell, "The New Uncertainty Principle," *Scientific American*, January 2001, 18–19.

4. M. Csikszentmihalyi, *Finding Flow: The Psychology of Engagement with Everyday Life* (New York: Basic Books, 1997), p. 101.

5. Ibid., p. 33.

6. P. Howard, *The Death of Common Sense: How Law Is Suffocating America* (New York: Random House, 1994).

7. T. Petzinger, "Mexican Cement Firm Decides to Mix Chaos into Company Strategy," *Wall Street Journal*, 13 December 1996, B1, 4.

8. Ibid., B1.

9. P. Katel, "Bordering on Chaos," *Wired*, July 1997, 98–107.

10. K.E. Weick and F. Westley, "Organizational Learning: Affirming an Oxymoron," *Handbook of Organizational Studies*, eds. S. Clegg, C. Hardy, and W. Nord (London: Sage, 1996), 440–458.

PART II

EMBRACING THE CHALLENGE

6

HOW CAN YOU "EMBRACE UNCERTAINTY?"

In the high country of the mind one has to become
adjusted to the thinner air of uncertainty,
and to the enormous magnitude of questions asked,
and the answers proposed to these questions.
The sweep goes on and on and on
so obviously much further than the mind can grasp
one hesitates even to go near for fear of getting lost in them
and never finding one's way out.
—*Robert Pirsig*

Some people respond to the "embrace uncertainty" philosophy by asking, "Don't you need *some* certainty in your life?" Of course you do. We have been careful to avoid a full-scale assault on certainty. Clearly, you need some degree of closure in order to move forward. Our concern, though, lies with the *balance* between the forces for certainty and uncertainty. Both have their place, but the scale is out of whack: Certainty-producing tools weigh in on decisions more than they should.

The Model

Figure 6.1 provides a way to visualize the tensions that leaders must manage. A wave-like rhythm of crests of uncertainty and troughs of certainty suggests a way to continually progress and meet ever-changing challenges. Wise leaders understand how the relationship between the crests and troughs provides the essential tension for meaningful progress; in a dynamic climate, the seas are seldom flat.

Two basic activities govern whether you are moving toward certainty or uncertainty. *Exploring* increases uncertainty as you reach out for new possibilities. *Refining* increases certainty as you further develop an existing idea, endeavor, or approach. A *platform* represents a relatively stable bundle of notions, activities, or decisions that provides a foundation or springboard from which to act. Consider a software package (1.1), for example. Subsequent *versions* (1.2, 1.3, etc.) of the software represent incremental improvements of the platform and a move toward greater certainty. A new platform (2.1) indicates a radical or quantum leap forward, which almost always means a jump into greater uncertainty. *Progress* occurs as you move from left to right and may happen in either the refining or exploring modes.[1]

Key Concepts of the Model

To fully appreciate the utility of this model, we need to clarify a few concepts.

Exploring

Explorers are masters of discovery and observation. Exploring skills increase uncertainty and involve a number of important activities:

- Networking—making useful connections with other people or ideas;
- Dreaming—imagining the possibilities;
- Scanning—quickly, systematically, and strategically surveying the situation;

Figure 6.1   **Uncertainty Management Model**

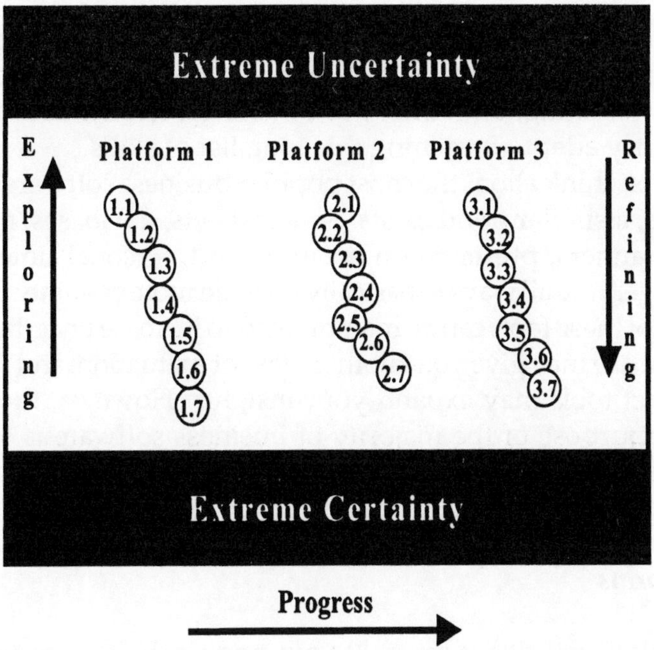

- Brainstorming—developing a lot of ideas to solve problems;
- Developing synchronicity—learning how to look at the world in terms of relationships rather than a bunch of "things";[2]
- Experimenting—systematically testing ideas or plans; and
- "Surfing" the World Wide Web.

Frankly, this list seems inadequate. Maybe that is because there has been so little research on the essential skills needed to be a good explorer. Exploring includes "brainstorming" but goes way beyond it. Explorers seek more than novel ideas; they create unusual relationships, foster deeper insights, and simultaneously work in many dimensions.

Refining

Refining skills increase certainty and include planning, organizing, delegating, project managing, scheduling, financial forecasting, and a host of others. Generally, educators are fairly adept at teaching this long list of skills.

If you think about the most popular business software programs, a similar trend exists: Spreadsheets, databases, meeting planners, presentation creators, and personal financial managers are all ways to basically provide more certainty. Sure, some of these tools can be manipulated to increase uncertainty; a database may give you another view of a situation, and some Internet tools may expand your insights. However, the primary purpose of the majority of business software is to increase certainty, providing further evidence that certainty gets a lot more attention than uncertainty.

Platforms

The platform idea is central to our approach. It represents a closely coupled bundle of notions, activities, or decisions that provides a foundation or springboard from which to act. It is, in effect, a temporary resting spot for your knowledge. Some examples:

- a first draft of a proposal;
- a phase of a building project;
- a job position;
- a computer chip design;
- a theory.

In Figure 6.1, we represent the platform with a series of circles signifying the general shaping of a notion. Platforms provide order, direct attention, and mold responses. Different versions emerge through further refinements, which we represent with a series of trailing circles (1.1, 1.2, 1.3, etc.). For instance, the first draft of this book was a platform. We had all the basic ideas, but we knew what issues needed further development, and every subsequent revision was based on the first draft. Without that platform we could speculate forever about how to "embrace uncertainty." We had to have a place to start; it was one of many potential beginning points, but the platform, as shaky as it was, provided the initial focus necessary to complete the project. In this way the first draft or "platform 1.1" shaped our responses, ordered our world, and directed our attention to critical issues. Like the series of overlapping circles, our final draft on this platform (1.9) was based on subsequent refinements of the first draft.

Once a platform has been created, there are two possibilities: (a) further develop the existing platform or (b) use it as a springboard to develop another platform. In either case, exploring or refining might be useful. For instance, assume that an employee wants to learn how to construct a newsletter. Consider two options that she entertains:

1. She can learn how to make her current word processing package do the necessary gyrations. In essence, by *refining* she further develops this existing skill platform.
2. On the other hand, she can search for the latest "newsletter" software package and move away from an existing certainty by *exploring* other options. Thus, she would create another platform.

Clearly, the decision to further develop an existing platform or build a new one is not always an easy one to make. For example, when writing this book, we completely refocused the manuscript in midstream to reflect our ongoing research and new audience. After having completed version 1.9 of the manuscript, we realized we had to make a tough choice and create a new platform (2.1) for subsequent revisions. In making that decision, we fully recognized that we would have to progress through the same refinement process that we experienced in platform 1.

Implications

There are many implications of this model that are explored in other chapters. However, we highlight a few below.

First, There Is an Optimum Point of Uncertainty

Yes, it is possible to have too much uncertainty. To continue to explore without a point of consolidation indicates an unwillingness or inability to make critical judgments and arrive at any sense of closure.

When Thomas Edison was conducting experiments to find the perfect filament for a lightbulb, he periodically took stock of the general class of materials that worked and those that did not. The folklore surrounding Edison's amazing discovery usually focuses on his persistence at testing hundreds of materials. But, that is only half the story.[3] Persistence without reflection *may* eventually yield results, but persistence coupled with contemplation *hastens* the speed of innovation. Edison's genius lies in his ability to use his exploratory failures to learn about the next step. William James explained it this way: "To be fertile in hypothesis is the first requisite, and to be willing to throw them away the moment experience contradicts them is the next."[4]

Detecting the optimum point of uncertainty often proves difficult. We would like to provide absolutely clear signposts indicating when you reach this point. But we can't. Think of the problem a horticulturist faces when advising clients about how much water a houseplant needs. At what point have you over-watered the plant? A cactus takes less than an ivy, but it is difficult to be more precise. Likewise, the optimal degree of uncertainty varies from issue to issue. However, we can provide some general guidelines:

- You may have gone too far when you create consensus at such an abstract level that it is functionally meaningless. For instance, we heard an academic discussion of "quality" that was intellectually engaging but of little practical utility.
- Another signal is that you ignore survival signs. Some adventure-seekers go too far and imperil their own safety by climbing the mountain in treacherous conditions. You might have a sense of drift.
- Going off on a tangent may be helpful, but going off on a tangent from the tangent may be problematic. Once again, this is a tricky matter since some sense of drift may actually be useful, but a prolonged one can be problematic.

Out of necessity, we are being a bit vague. Through experience, wise leaders develop a keen sense of the danger signals as they approach the optimum point of uncertainty.

Second, There Is an Optimum Point of Certainty

The optimal amount of certainty is also difficult to specify, yet the danger signs are somewhat easier to detect. A mad rush toward perfection should send up a red flag, like trying to nail down every detail for an impending organizational change. Similarly, a concerted drive toward a single solution can signal that you are crossing the line. Whenever you encounter resistance to further exploration, you may also be nearing the line. The opposition to further inquiry sometimes is vocalized using this delightfully, circular reasoning:

> Person A: We've got to stick to the plan because it's the plan.
> Person B: Why don't you change the plan?
> Person A: It's the plan; you can't change it.

This loopy logic instills a sense a certainty amidst the pressures imposed by rapidly changing events. The artificial certainty dissipates in the face of clear failure, but unclear thinking often abides: "I don't know what went wrong. . . . I followed the plan." Sadly, individuals caught in this trap rarely appreciate that their own needs for certainty lie at the root of their failure.

Third, No Platform Is Perfect

Platforms are constructed and maintained in a sea of uncertainty. Their primary function is to provide some stability amidst the tumult. For instance, when Microsoft rolled out Windows 95, many hailed it as a major milestone. Why? In the most basic sense, it provided fairly simple and straightforward solutions to a vast sea of user problems. In particular, users could navigate on a computer without reference to an arcane list of commands, a problem many Mac users gleefully retorted that they never had. Mac users had a delicious rejoinder to the Windows 95 hoopla: "Windows 95 = Mac 80."

The retort was delightful, but beside the point. Windows 95 provided a useful, though not perfect, platform for users of IBM and IBM-compatible machines. Minor flaws were continually discovered and then corrected. Interestingly, Microsoft did not anticipate the importance of the Internet at that time. As a result, Windows 95 was not a particularly effective way to seize those opportunities. Consequently, in later years Microsoft devoted considerable technical and legal resources into constructing other operating system platforms that were more Internet-friendly.

A platform does not have to be perfect to be successful; it just needs to solve the problems of today and on the immediate horizon. It provides enough certainty to launch further inquiries. Isaac Newton's theories provided a platform of understanding that allowed Einstein to create an even more encompassing platform, and it is safe to say that someday, someone will use Einstein's platform to create another one.

Physicists of all generations know the importance of dynamic stability. The concept works equally well in describing the power of platforms. The stability of a platform increases in each successive version (1.1, 1.2, etc.). The dynamism of the system emerges from successive jumps between the platforms (1.7 to 2.1 and 2.7 to 3.1). Wise leaders know this and instinctively discern when their organization can further refine an existing platform or move to another one.[5]

Some people do not view platforms as temporary resting spots for knowledge. They find security on the platform and often resist leaving it. In fact, highly adaptable platforms may become problematic. When do you stop making home improvements and decide that you need an entirely new home? These decisions are always tough ones, and people may, therefore, stay on the platform too long. As Tim Mannon, an executive with Hewlett Packard, said, "The biggest single threat to our business today is staying with a previously successful business model one year too long."[6] A platform is not a retirement home.

Fourth, Progressing from One Platform to Another Provides the Implicit Measure of Effectiveness

On May 25, 1961, President John F. Kennedy challenged the United States to put a man on the moon and return him safely to earth "before the decade is out." On July 16, 1969, Neil Armstrong stood on lunar soil. This was one of the most spectacular success stories of the modern era. How did it happen?

At the heart of the process lies the adroit management of uncertainty by establishing viable platforms from which to explore and refine. With the Mercury program, NASA refined techniques that allowed men to function while weightless. The Mercury platform set the stage for the Gemini program, which in turn was transformed into the platform for the Apollo program. After six Mercury flights, ten Gemini flights, and four Apollo flights, the mission was accomplished: "One small step for [a] man, one giant leap for mankind." This is a quintessential example of how uncertainty can be safely embraced. It reminds us of philosopher Robert Grudin's thought-provoking maxim, ". . . the only thing forbidden should be to stand still and say, 'This is it.'"[7] Successful organizations look beyond today's platform and envision the possibilities.

On a similar note, Will Rogers once observed, "Even if you are on the right track, you'll get run over if you sit still." His witty remarks should subtly lure you into considering some profound questions:

- How long do you stay with a platform that is meeting your needs?
- When have you learned enough to build a new platform?
- What should be the relationship between the old platform and the new one?

Grappling with these issues addresses the notion of effectiveness at the most fundamental level.

Progress does not necessarily equate with the amount of time spent refining a platform. To paraphrase Picasso, "Every act of creation is first of all an act of destruction of existing platforms." Constructing the perfect Mercury space capsule would not have put a man on the moon. Excellence is achieved by moving from one less-than-perfect platform to a better one. Note that in Figure 6.2, line A is shorter than line B, indicating that typically you make more progress by jumping into the uncertainty and establishing new platforms than by merely refining an existing structure. The price of excellence, then, is an abiding sense of incompleteness.

Fifth, the Perception of the Amount of Uncertainty Is Directly Related to the Platform on Which You Stand

There is a great deal of uncertainty to conquer when looking at the Kennedy challenge from the Mercury platform

Figure 6.2 **Measuring Progress and Perception with the Uncertainty Management Model**

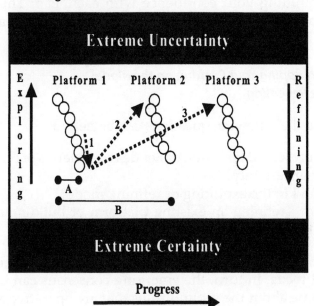

(see line 3 in Figure 6.2). The number of exploring/refining cycles appears less daunting when viewed from the vantage point of the first Apollo flights. Thus, the platforms help to temper the natural anxiety associated with great uncertainty. Clearly, the move from version 1.6 to 1.7 is less traumatic than a jump to a new platform (compare lines 1 and 2 in Figure 6.2). However, jumping across too many platforms too quickly appears to be a daunting task (see line 3 in Figure 6.2). The "giant leap for mankind" was made possible by thoughtfully stepping from platform to platform, each one decreasing the perceived uncertainty of the momentous undertaking. This idea can be particularly helpful in learning to embrace uncertainty: You don't have to embrace all the uncertainty at once (line 3); rather, you can deal with chunks of it at a time (line 2). You then learn more about the uncertainty associated with the challenge. You also enhance your skills of dealing with uncertainty in general, building your confidence with each leap. This skill and confidence will become increasingly important as you reach borders of your own understanding.

Sixth, Mapping Your Position on the Model Can Be Revealing

Asking the following questions can be helpful:

- How would I position our endeavor in terms of certainty or uncertainty?
- Am I in the exploring or refining mode?
- Am I refining an existing platform or building a new one?

Debating these questions in a group setting provides a sound focus. In turn, the emerging consensus can inform everyone about the ground rules that are operative at that point in time. For instance, you may be more comfortable in the refining mode. Knowing that the discussion is moving to an exploratory phase may decrease your frustration level. You will also develop a sense of who is more effective at exploring and refining. You might discover, as others have, that a symphony conductor's gesture can signal a crescendo into uncertainty or a decrescendo into certainty. Thus, you can shape the cacophony of voices into a more harmonious discussion.

Mapping a group's position on the model may also signal some potential problems, such as:

Tug-of-War

Some group members are exploring while others are refining (see Figure 6.3a). The net result is that the full benefits of either exploring or refining are not reaped. Instead a weird and untenable compromise is often reached.

Figure 6.3a **Tug-of-War**

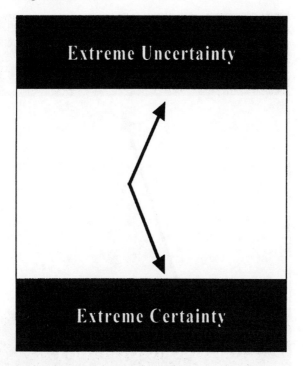

Never-Ending Mountain Climb

The group tends to explore the possibilities for long periods of time (see Figure 6.3b). These discussions are often at such high levels of abstraction that, in the end, very little is accomplished. The conversations of academics frequently follow this path, partially explaining why many universities are so slow to respond to change.

Never-Ending Ski Slope

The group spends too much time refining proposals and hashing out all the details (see Figure 6.3c). Plateaus of reasonable certainty are not established. Meanwhile, the oppor-

Figure 6.3b **Never-Ending Mountain Climb**

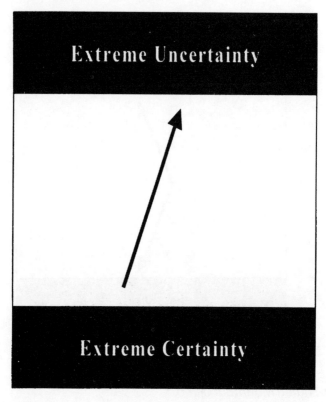

tunity passes. Perfecting the greatest pet rock or hula-hoop is not a wise investment of time. By the time the products are perfected, the craze has passed.

Note that neither conflict nor collaboration is necessarily a sign that something has gone awry. Conflict can be problematic if part of the group is heading in one direction and part in another. Yet conflict can be helpful if used as a signal to ask, "Should we be exploring or refining right now or should we be moving to a new platform?" Agreements based on the discussion of this question can be useful. However, a group that unconsciously collaborates to explore or refine for extended periods can be equally problematic. Platforms

Figure 6.3c **Never-Ending Ski Slope**

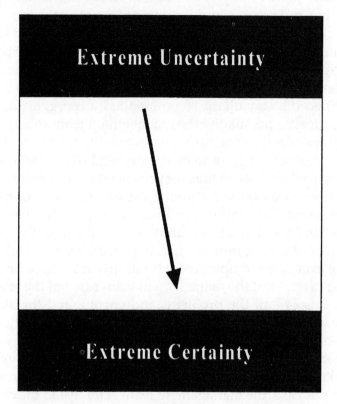

are not established, and opportunities are not seized. Thus, monitoring your position on the model provides a wonderful tool to spark important discussions.

Finally, Effective Leaders Intuitively Discern When to Engage Others in Exploring and Refining

Employees in one medical clinic typically greeted major changes with a mixture of incredulity, fear, and resistance. The office climate was stifling, processes were inefficient, and frustration was high. The management team was frustrated because the staff did not follow through on the "well-crafted" plans. They spent a great deal of time perfecting existing procedures and issuing orders to make sure they were followed. In essence, the management team did all the exploring and refining. The staff did neither but was expected to execute the finely honed plans. A consultant noticed this pattern and believed it was part of the underlying problem.

When the consultant recommended a reorganization of the office, he persuaded the management team to approach the impending restructuring in a very different way than in the past. Instead of announcing detailed plans and expecting everyone to fall in line, they resolved to actively embrace uncertainty by only discussing the general aims of the restructuring. The entire staff initially shaped the plans and remolded them as events unfolded. To be sure, this was a messier planning process than they used before. And there were even a few employees who simply wanted to be "told what to do." But the management team resisted the temptation to solve all the problems and encouraged the staff to find workable solutions within the framework of the general objectives. The result: the smoothest transition in clinic history. There were fewer staff complaints, the systems worked more efficiently, and patient satisfaction increased.

In this case, the management team actively led the change by deftly shifting between exploring and refining. This was no easy task. It required a fundamental shift in leadership style from one of *directing activity* to one of *framing challenges*. There was, however, an added bonus. A year later, when the clinic approached another major change, they had the skill and confidence to quickly respond to the challenge. By embracing uncertainty, the clinic fostered flexibility.

Concluding Thoughts

Thus far, we have discussed how to embrace uncertainty on a theoretical level. The remaining chapters focus on a more practical level. Our strategy is simple and straightforward:

· Cultivate an awareness of uncertainty (Chapter 7).
· Process the uncertainty (Chapter 8).
· Catalyze action during uncertain times (Chapter 9).

Each component of the strategy reinforces the others, building a cycle designed to maximize the benefits of the uncertainty inherent in our world. Leaders and organizations that master this cycle know how to properly balance the virtues of the certainty- and uncertainty-producing tools, thereby creating the dynamic climate that energizes and invigorates employees.

Notes

1. Our diagram doesn't picture it, but it is possible that a new version or platform does not result in progress.

2. For more details on this concept, see J. Jaworski, *Synchronicity: The Inner Path of Leadership* (San Francisco: Berrett-Koehler, 1998).

3. N. Baldwin, *Edison: Inventing the Century* (New York: Hyperion, 1995).

4. Ibid., p. 128.

5. E. Abrahamson, "Change Without Pain," *Harvard Business Review* 78, no. 4 (2000): 75–82.

6. R. Hoff, "Hewlett Packard," *Business Week*, 13 February 1995, 67.

7. R. Grudin, *Time and the Art of Living* (New York: Ticknor & Fields, 1982) , p. 2.

7

HOW CAN YOU CULTIVATE AN AWARENESS OF UNCERTAINTY?

*In times of change the learners will inherit the earth,
while the knowers will find themselves beautifully equipped
for a world that no longer exists.
—Eric Hoffer*

Our research revealed that leaders and organizations embrace uncertainty by mastering three basic competencies (see Figure 7.1):

- Cultivating an awareness of uncertainty.
- Processing (e.g., communicating) the uncertainty.
- Catalyzing action in an uncertain environment.

Often these three activities must occur simultaneously. Knowing when to jump across the levels requires both experience and considerable mental flexibility. This means that plans are constantly in flux, the rules of the game may vary from day-to-day, and leaders must quickly determine when it is time to change the approach. This is like the quarterback who has studied the training films and has called the play, but then realizes at the line of scrimmage that he should call an audible to change the play. He *cultivated an awareness* of the uncertainties while watching the game tapes, *processed the alternatives* in the huddle, and *catalyzed action* according to the dictates of the situation.

Figure 7.1   **Uncertainty Management Competencies**

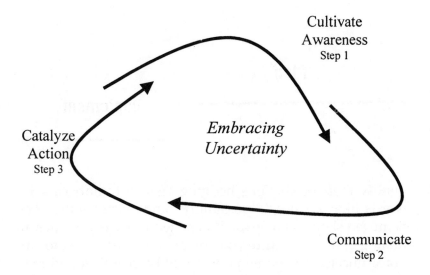

This model departs from the traditional approach to decision making (see Figure 7.2). Typically, leaders are taught to plan first and then to implement the plan. Organizations using this approach often lack the flexibility to rapidly adapt to changing conditions, just like the quarterback who sticks with the play regardless of the defensive alignment. Our approach emphasizes *dynamic* movement across the three levels. We explore each of these competencies in this chapter as well as in Chapters 8 and 9.

Misconceptions

Fretting about the local weather forecast is a seemingly innocuous pastime. We all have heard friends lamenting that "You can't trust a thing they say anyway" or "What do they know?" Yet weather forecasters are one of the few professionals that really imbue their talk with uncertainty. They

Figure 7.2   **Traditional Management of Uncertainty**

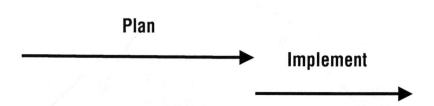

qualify their predictions hedging against tomorrow with words like "chance," "possibility" and "probability." The bemused skepticism heaped on meteorologists provides an inkling of the adventure you embark on when trying to embrace uncertainty. Some people will be skeptical and may even mock you. After all, most people want certainty. But take comfort. Of all those in the prediction business—including economists, market gurus, and futurists—by far the most accurate are weather forecasters.[1] One reason is that they freely acknowledge their ignorance in the face of enormous complexity and randomness. You must have a special mindset to break the spell of certainty. In this section we dispel the myths that may inhibit people from experiencing the peculiar magic of uncertainty.

Misconception 1: Failure Is Harmful

The fear of failure may be the greatest barrier to embracing uncertainty. It discourages people from looking at a situation from different angles. It prevents them from trying something new. And it hinders progress. In sum, it inhibits natural curiosity and quenches the exploratory spirit. Intellectually, you may know that failure is just part of the learning experience. After all everyone takes some spills before they learn to ride a bike. Over time their willingness to take those spills diminishes. Why? Perhaps the desire to feel competent takes over the desire to explore and learn. Ironically, when you stop exploring, your competence begins to wane.

Michael Jordan, arguably the greatest basketball player of all time, has an interesting perspective:

> If it turns out my best isn't good enough, then at least I'll never be able to look back and say I was too afraid to try. Maybe I just didn't have it. Maybe I just wasn't good enough. There's nothing wrong with that and nothing to be afraid of either. Failure always made me try harder the next time. That's why my advice has always been to "think positive" and find fuel in any failure. Sometimes failure actually gets you closer to where you want to be.[2]

His mental balance sheet is revealing. Instead of thinking about the costs of failure, he thinks about the potential regrets of not trying. Legendary basketball coach John Wooden may have reconceptualized the issue best when he said, "failure is never fatal; failure to change might be."

Misconception 2: Consistency Is Always Important

True sports fans want the referees to make consistent calls for both teams. Each team gets the same penalty for the same infraction. This only seems fair. Our sense of fairness springs from this principle: When situations are similar, the same rules should apply to everyone. But when events are spread over time, and circumstances are constantly changing, does this principle still apply? We don't think so. An over-emphasis on consistency may force people to see a similarity between two situations and blind them to dissimilarity. For instance, there were many pundits who predicted that the Gulf War would be another Vietnam War. Contemplating his illustrious career as a high-ranking official in the Israeli government, Abba Eban observed: "Consistency amid the ebb and flow of crises is an advanced form of intellectual sloth. It replaces empirical wisdom by dogmatic fallacy."[3] The drive for consistency has a way of artificially providing certainty by stripping away the important situational differences that make each event unique. Thus, our reconceptualization is: Understanding the uniqueness of experience is more important than consistency.

Misconception 3: Answers Are More Important Than Questions

When you focus on getting all the answers correct, you are, in fact, limiting your knowledge. Consider the Chinese notion of knowledge. It is composed of two ideographs, one representing "learning," the other, "questioning" (see Figure 7.3).

People who fixate on "getting all the facts" often forget the other essential component of knowledge: Learning the significant questions. If you want to embrace uncertainty, then you need to also focus on developing the right questions. The answers you discover are directly tied to the questions you ask. If you are asking the wrong question, you may get the right answer but the wrong insight. For instance, management expert Peter Drucker made the notable distinction between effectiveness and efficiency.[4] Someone posing an efficiency question asks, "Are you doing things the right way?" A person inquiring about effectiveness asks, "Are you doing the right things?" It is entirely possible to be very efficient while being completely ineffective. In this way, the questions people ask may limit their success.

Questions implicitly allow you to embrace uncertainty while simultaneously providing focus by shaping your inquiry. When people explore those answers together, they open themselves to novelty, nuance, and knowledge. Insightful questions encourage people to reevaluate their implicit thinking patterns. In order to ask these kinds of questions, you need to know what is not known.[5] In other words, in-

Figure 7.3 **Chinese Characters for Knowledge**

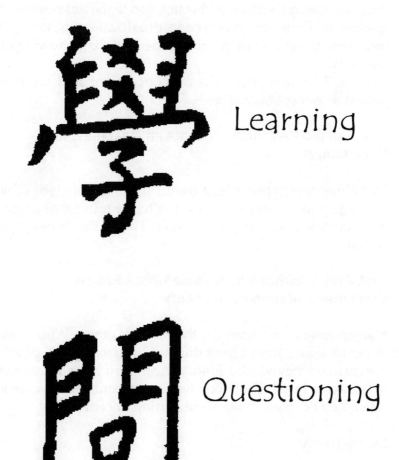

dividuals need to come face-to-face with their own ignorance and confusion. A trivia question focuses on the known, but the profound question directs attention to the unknown and uncertain. Therefore, our reconceptualization is: Asking a profound question can be more beneficial than knowing all the facts.

Table 7.1 summarizes the misconceptions and the suggested reconceptualizations.

How Can You Personally Cultivate an Awareness of Uncertainty?

Dispelling myths provides a useful starting point (see Table 7.1). The path forward, however, often requires that people develop new skills and sensibilities. That is the focus of this section.

First, Seek Inspiration from Those Whose Success Came from Embracing Uncertainty

Many people are reassured by the words of others. When seeking emotional support for a difficult or lonely quest, people turn to those they admire. Embracing uncertainty often proves to be such a quest. Therefore, we have recorded below some celebrated peoples' thoughts regarding uncertainty.

Charles Handy

Charles Handy, a former oil company executive, successful author, and professor at the London School of Business, discussed an important, personally defining moment:

> When I went to school, I did not learn anything much that I now remember; except for this hidden message, that every major problem in life had already been solved. . . . The aim of education, in that world of certainty, was to transfer the answers from the teacher to me, by one means or another. It was a crippling

Table 7.1

Common Misconceptions

Misconception	Reconception
Failure is harmful.	Failure is never fatal, failure to change might be.
Consistency is always important.	Understanding the uniqueness of experience is more important than consistency.
Answers are more important than questions.	Asking a profound question can be more beneficial than knowing all the facts.

assumption. For years afterward, when confronted with a problem that was new to me, I ran for an expert. It never occurred to me, in that world of certainty, that some problems were new, or that I might come up with my own answers. I was continually downskilling myself. I was also cheating myself of my potential.[6]

John Hagel

John Hagel, the head of McKinsey & Company's Worldwide Interactive Multimedia Practice, was asked about how companies can stay alive and even thrive in the Internet age. He responded:

Companies attempting to survive, much less prosper, in these new environments are going to be ill-served by traditional business-school notions—get a clear view of the endgame, focus on the migration path, then position yourself in that endgame. What happens if the endgame is unknowable, as it will be? Now what do you do? . . . Traditional management reaction to high uncertainty is "I want to maximize control," whereas the real operating principle here is, "Don't try to control everything. Share the risk. Get others involved."[7]

Eleanor Roosevelt

President Franklin D. Roosevelt's wife, Eleanor Roosevelt, could have enjoyed a quiet life basking in the reflected glow of her husband's political career. But she didn't. She was a social activist, championing women's and minority's rights long before it became fashionable to do so. After FDR's death, she became a delegate to the United Nations. She was a remarkable person who overcame personal heartbreak as well as a natural shyness. Her life and words inspired millions. Her philosophy of life was a quintessential example of someone who embraced uncertainty. Consider these thoughtful comments:

> Never, perhaps, have any of us needed as much as we do today to use all the curiosity we have, needed to seek new knowledge, needed to realize that no knowledge is terminal. For almost everything in our world is new, startlingly new. None of us can afford to stop learning or to check our curiosity about new things, or to lose our humility in the face of new situations. If we can keep that flexibility of mind, that hospitality toward new ideas, we will be able to welcome the new flow of thought wherever it comes, not resisting it; weighing and evaluating and exploring the strange new concepts that confront us at every turn. We cannot shut the windows and pull down the shades; we cannot say, "I have learned all I need to know; my opinions are fixed on everything. I refuse to change or consider these new things." Not today. Not any more.[8]

She penned these words in the waning years of her life in the aptly titled book *You Learn by Living*. Today's leaders can still learn much from her.

Second, Develop an Aesthetic Appreciation for Chaotic Environments

Those who embrace uncertainty often have an aesthetic appreciation of chaotic environments such as an avalanche or the operation of stock markets. What intrigues them is finding the fundamental pattern amid all the confusion. They view the complexity as a challenge and see beauty in the chaos. Instead of labeling the environment as confusing, they think about the preponderance of possibilities. Merely surrounding yourself with complex images can help you become a connoisseur of chaos. For example, some people enjoy pondering fractals. [9] These are exquisitely complex images based on simple underlying formulas; simplicity and complexity are at once distant and near (see Figure 7.4).

Third, Peruse Different Maps of the Same Territory

When you try this exercise, you will probably notice that one map may have a road that another does not have. One map may show a route to a destination that the other does not. One map may picture all the fast food restaurants while another, the bike trails. Thus, all maps are incomplete; they focus on some aspects of the territory while ignoring others. Maps appear to be objective and factual but they are not. Professor of Geography Mark Monmonier put it this way: "Subtle cartographic propaganda is common in many contexts and frequently misleads citizens who are unaware that maps are highly selective and necessarily biased."[10] Similar to planning documents, with their step-by-step procedures and checklists, therefore, maps only *appear* to provide certainty. Leaders need to be able to draw more than one map of a territory; they need to imagine options other than the single one created by the certainty provider.

Fourth, Change Your Physical Environment

People have a way of ordering their intellectual, social, and physical surroundings so as to drive out the chaos. They know where things are located. They have ready access to information and tools. They rarely stumble into the unexpected. They even have a pretty good idea who they will encounter in many social situations. Changing their surroundings upsets their conventions and creates more opportunities for serendipitous experiences. It allows them to

Figure 7.4 **Fractal**

Note: Dr. Peter Breznay of the University of Wisconsin-Green Bay created this fractal using the following formula:

$$z_{n+1} = \cosh^2(z_n) + c$$

"practice" dealing with uncertain situations, creating confidence amidst the sea of chaos.

There are a variety of ways to change your surroundings. One approach that some companies have adopted involves developing highly flexible work spaces. Some ideas, like using a small suitcase on wheels to substitute for a desk, may seem a bit bizarre. Other innovations, such as tables on wheels, easily movable partitions, and more open office landscaping, often prove liberating. So says the prestigious

Fraunhofer Institute research group in Germany that runs the "office innovation center." People become less "turf conscious," communication improves, and teams more easily flow to the work.[11] It makes sense because in these office environments, change requires less energy on both a physical and psychological level. International Business Machines experimented with such ideas and discovered that they also reduced costs. Many of those who change their physical environment tend to be resourceful, adaptive, and flexible. Their spirits are actually motivated by the possibilities. They smile when they say, "I don't always know what's going to happen next."

Fifth, Modify Your Communication Style

How leaders speak has a powerful way of structuring their worldview. Those who typically talk in bipolar terms tend to create a world full of artificial certainty. For instance, a manager who insists that employees either *accept* or *reject* his plan discourages the creation of alternative plans. Yet the manager who says, "If we assume X, then I think this plan is best," has created an opportunity to modify the plan should employees feel different assumptions are operative. Even this minor stylistic change can open the door to some uncertainty. Table 7.2 presents some ways to communicate that cultivate uncertainty.

Metaphors also exert considerable, but tacit, influence on employees' tolerance for uncertainty. Contrast these statements:

- The wheels are set in motion; we will be at full production in a month.
- The plan should go off like clockwork.
- We don't see any storm clouds on the horizon. Our forecast is that we will be at full production in a month.

The first two statements allude to a machine metaphor. Machines are linear and predictable—the outcome is certain.[12]

Table 7.2

Communicating to Cultivate Uncertainty

Words to avoid	Alternatives
That's the way it is, period.	This is the way I see it.
The complete . . .	One of the answers is . . .
The final word on the subject is . . .	If we assume X, then Y follows.
My way or no way.	One alternative is . . .
This is the definitive answer.	This answer is based on these facts . . .

The last statement is based on a weather metaphor. The weather is dynamic and more fluid; the outcome less certain. If you are trying to reach a deadline, the machine metaphor might be best. If you are trying to prepare employees for a more uncertain world, the weather metaphor proves superior. In fact, when management makes a conscious effort to use the weather metaphor as opposed to certainty metaphors, their organizations experience some remarkable benefits. Employees temper their expectations and grow more willing to adapt to the unexpected. They become less dependent and committed to a single plan while cultivating greater sensitivity to business climate fluctuations. They are less disappointed when projections don't pan out, and they don't blame management. In summary: The words leaders use matter a great deal.

How Can You Get Your Organization to Embrace Uncertainty?

Effective leaders create a dynamic climate by crafting an environment in which uncertainty is not only recognized, but actually cultivated. Leaders can plant the right seeds by using the following strategies:

First, Occasionally "Shake the Platform"

"Platforms" represent the set of beliefs and practices about "how things are done best around here." Sometimes in the quest for certainty, employees get a little too comfortable. This is precisely the time to "shake the platform." Consequently, employees begin to think about the unknowns, complexities, ambiguities, and conflicting perspectives implicit in the status quo.

Consider the case of a senior executive who shook the platform during an off-site strategic planning meeting. For several days, one executive after another laid out the strategic plan for their division using well-crafted slides and highly organized notebooks. But this executive's handouts weren't in any particular order. He watched in amusement as the buzz around the room grew. "What order are these supposed to be in?" As he approached the podium, the murmurs faded, and he said:

> I watched what happened when I passed out the handouts. You wanted to know what section they went in. This is a perfect illustration of what I want to talk about today. The truth of the matter is that I don't know. No one knows the precise steps that we have to take to develop this new business. We *do not know* because we *cannot know* at this point. We know the general direction we want to go, but we simply can't provide you all the details at this time. So let me talk about our direction. . . .[13]

At the end of his presentation, someone raised his hand and asked, "I enjoyed your presentation, but what order *do* the handouts go in?" Clearly, sometimes the innate desire for certainty proves overwhelming for some folks.

Likewise, Bill Gates once told his software developers: "There's not a single line of code here today that will have value, say in four or five years' time."[14] That statement would rock the platform for even the most creative of persons. His message was abundantly clear: What are you learning today that we can use tomorrow?

Second, Challenge Existing Heuristics or Rules of Thumb

Organizations, like people, have fairly well-developed heuristics designed to reduce complexity. Unfortunately, these rules of thumb can lead to systematic thinking errors. Moreover, researchers have also determined that most people are over-confident in estimating the accuracy of their judgments.[15] Challenging existing heuristics can break the spell of over-confidence. For instance, conventional wisdom in the 1940s was that only the wealthy would invest in the stock market. Merrill Lynch tested that rule of thumb by deploying mobile brokerage offices in refurbished buses and marketing services to those on the "Main Streets" of cities and towns all across the land. Consequently, they built one of the largest and strongest brokerage businesses in the United States. That never would have happened without executives cultivating an awareness of uncertainty by challenging the existing heuristic.

Likewise, Stuart Kauffman, the chief scientist of Bios Group and a legitimate complexity guru, has used algorithms based on biological thinking to challenge existing rules of thumb in a variety of industries.[16] For instance, Procter & Gamble used to have a rule that required their trucks to be fully loaded before shipping out. The Bios Group found that this rule and several others were costly to the company. When Procter & Gamble changed the rule, they realized a 25 percent reduction in inventory. That's a pretty good return on investment for embracing a little uncertainty.[17]

Third, "Fuzzy Up" Your Expectations

One of the telltale signs that you have embraced uncertainty is indicated by the nature of your expectations. In an uncertain environment, expectations tend to be fuzzy. Your objectives may be clear, but the time line and methods may still be unclear. Consider Dr. Bob Rotella, who for twenty years was the Director of Sports Psychology at the University of Virginia and consulted with sports organizations such as the Pro Golf Association. He made this telling observation:

> If you want to stay the course, it will help if you can fall in love not with improvement, but with the process of improvement. Improvement is not something you can tightly control. It will come, but you can't decide when and how much you'll get better.[18]

Likewise, consider the case of a manufacturing plant that had enjoyed many years of stability, market dominance, and financial success. The industry was maturing, however, and the plant leadership recognized that in the near future they would be moving to a more uncertain environment. During the first few transitional years, the plant manager prepared his workers by consistently talking about the need to embrace uncertainty and become more flexible. The employees dutifully nodded their heads. But when the inevitable changes started, the leadership team was disappointed by employee responses. Employees wanted to know production schedules several months in advance and yearned for definitive parameters of their job duties. In other words, they craved all the certainty and stability associated with the past. Trust between management and workers started to break down. The general consensus was that management was either stupid (didn't know what was going on), helpless (couldn't do anything about the situation), or evil (purposely trying to make workers' lives difficult).

For several months the leadership team tried to attack the terrible triad with messages aimed at correcting misperceptions. All to no avail. Eventually they realized that these were not *intellectual* reactions but *emotional* ones. The employees were raising reasonable questions that had uncertain answers. The climate started to change when the plant manager told this particularly illuminating story during the routine quarterly employee meeting:

> Years ago, I used this forum to tell you about all the things we thought were going to happen in the next quarter. And I was often wrong. In fact, business usually got a lot better than we forecasted. We were constantly being surprised. We would end up adding a machine or jobs that we did not anticipate. I was not lying to you then, and I am not lying to you now. The only difference is that now when we predict something, it sometimes turns out to be worse than anticipated. Our accuracy rate is about the same. That does not mean we are helpless or stupid; we do not know because we *cannot* know. Instead we need to become more adaptable in order to manage a rapidly changing marketplace.[19]

The wonderful story framed the employees' current emotional reactions with events of the past by deftly linking past "surprises" with current "disappointments." The plant manager's brilliant rhetorical strategy simultaneously attacked the terrible triad while challenging workers to "fuzzy up" their expectations.

Fourth, Put an Information Perish Date on All Communications

The written word often carries an illusion of permanence. Many people cling to an idea far too long because they have seen it written down. There are, of course, some truths that are time-tested, but many ideas and facts do not stand the test of time. Milk spoils if not used within a given time period; information does, too. Placing an information perish tag (see Figure 7.5) on all communication serves as a constant reminder of the uncertainty inherent to most information. It pushes people to be less dependent on a single fact and focuses attention on longer-term trends.

Fifth, Ask Penetrating Questions

Richard Wurman, author of the best selling book *Information Anxiety*, is a highly successful "information architect." He also designed several innovative access guides to cities, as well as a new kind of atlas of the United States. His comments about asking questions are revealing:

> When you sell your expertise—whether to a boss, a client, or even a friend—you have a limited repertoire. On the other hand, when you sell your ignorance, when you sell your desire to learn something, to create and explore and navigate paths to knowledge—when you sell your *curiosity*—you sell from a bucket that's infinitely deep, that represents an unlimited repertoire. My expertise has always been my ignorance—my admission and my acceptance of not knowing. My work comes from questions, not from answers.[20]

Clearly, he attributes much of his success to his willingness and skill to ask penetrating questions.

The right question can unmask artificial certainty. Consider some of the following:

- What certainty level should we attach to that fact, projection, or idea?
- Is it really possible to find an answer to that question?
- Do we really need to know all this before proceeding?
- Can we draw another map of the same situation?
- Is there another way to organize the ideas?
- Are we rushing to a decision?

Answers to these questions have a way of introducing more doubt into conversations. It may even foment some temporary confusion, which is another way of increasing the uncertainty.

Most people probe for details, proof, and counterarguments by asking questions such as, "What evidence do

Figure 7.5   **Information Perishability Tag**

you have to support that idea?" These are ways to increase certainty. When creating uncertainty, your probes should be directed at different targets. There are two ways to do this: direct and indirect probing.[21] A direct probe, such as "tell me more about what makes you uneasy about this idea," focuses attention on the intuition or hunch. Using vague words like "uneasy" or "uncomfortable" invites speculation. An indirect probe such as "Uh-huh . . ." or "I see . . ." can encourage people to continue talking about the matter. Either method can be useful, but the key is to focus attention on the intuition or unspoken rules of thumb. This means that vagaries, inconsistencies, and incomplete musings will actually enrich discussion. They must not only be tolerated

Table 7.3

Different Approaches to Probing

Probing for certainty	Probing for uncertainty
What evidence do you have to support that idea?	What makes you uneasy about this idea?
How are we going to implement that plan?	What image does this idea bring to mind?
Isn't your idea inconsistent with the plan?	If we threw away the plan, what would you propose?
Haven't you contradicted your earlier position?	If you were to place a bet on one of these options, which one would you pick?

but encouraged. You are not looking for the "right answer" only partially developed insights. Table 7.3 provides examples of the two different approaches to probing.

Sixth, Monitor the Environment

Perhaps the most fundamental survival skill in an uncertain environment is effectively monitoring changes. Only a foolish sailor expects the wind to always blow from one direction. Indeed, certainty-providers often create a false sense of security by decreasing the organization's watchfulness for relevant changes in the environment. In contrast, a reliable monitor warns of shifting winds. For a manager, it may mean taking into account subtle shifts in another department's role. For an organization, it may mean astutely assessing changes in the marketplace. The bottom line: Monitoring encourages organizations to make quick adjustments to the new contingencies.

Concluding Thoughts

Yesterday is one of the most beloved of all the songs composed by the Beatles. The beautifully plaintive melody connects to everyone's longings for harmony and peace. The words speak to yearnings for contentment and tranquility. Yet at a deeper level, the song stirs a passion for certainty. Yesterday represents the known. People know the joy of their past accomplishments. They even know the familiar sweetness of heartaches survived. Their emotional comfort with the past often inhibits them from fully embracing the possibilities of the future. Tomorrow beckons with the unknown, the uncertain. Yet, when leaders dispel troubling misconceptions and hone their skills, they can transform the dreams of today into the accomplishments of tomorrow.

Notes

1. W.A. Sherden, *The Fortune Sellers: The Big Business of Buying and Selling Predictions* (New York: John Wiley, 1998). Also see J.L. Casti, *Searching For Certainty: What Scientists Can Know About the Future* (New York: William Morrow, 1990).

2. M. Jordan, *I Can't Accept Not Trying: Michael Jordan On the Pursuit of Excellence* (New York: HarperSanFrancisco, 1994), p. 10.

3. A. Eban, *Personal Witness: Israel Through My Eyes* (New York: G.P. Putnam, 1992), p. 655.

4. P. Drucker, *Management: Tasks, Responsibilities, and Practices* (New York: Harper & Row, 1974).

5. N. Miyake and D.A. Norman, "To Ask a Question, One Must Know Enough to Know What Is Not Known," *Journal of Verbal Learning and Verbal Behavior* 18, no. 2 (1979): 357–364.

6. C. Handy, *Beyond Certainty: The Changing World of Organizations* (Boston: Harvard Business School Press, 1996), pp. 16–17.

7. K. Kelly, "It Takes a Village to Make a Mall: Net Gain's John Hagel on the Prerequisite for Net Commerce Community," *Wired*, August 1997, 84–86.

8. E. Roosevelt, *You Learn by Living* (New York: Harper & Brothers, 1960), p. 16.

9. B. Mandelbrot, *The Fractal Geometry of Nature* (New York: W.H. Freeman, 1983).

10. M. Monmonier, *Drawing the Line: Tales of Maps Cartocontroversy* (New York: Henry Holt, 1995), p. 297.

11. D. Aalund, "German Group Sets Vision for the Office of the Future," *Wall Street Journal*, 30 October 2000, B12.

12. G. Morgan, *Images of Organization* (Newbury Park, CA: Sage, 1986).

13. Interview with P. Clampitt, 11 May 2000, source wishes to remain anonymous.

14. R.E. Stross, *The Microsoft Way: The Real Story of How the Company Outsmarts Its Competition* (Reading, MA: Addison-Wesley, 1997), p. 36.

15. J.E. Russo and P.J. Schoemaker, "Managing Overconfidence," *Sloan Management Review* 33, no. 2 (1992): 7–17.

16. S. Kauffman, *At Home in the Universe* (New York: Oxford University Press, 1995).

17. G. Bylinsky, "Look Who's Doing R&D," *Fortune*, 27 November 2000, pp. 232C–V. Also see, J. Wakefield, "Complexity's Business Model," *Scientific American*, January 2001, 31–34.

18. B. Rotella, *The Golf of Your Dreams* (New York: Simon & Schuster, 1997), p. 131.

19. T. Cashman, interview with P. Clampitt, 5 April 2000.

20. R. Wurman, "Wurman Out Loud," *Inc.*, May 1997, 62.

21. C.W. Downs, G.P. Smeyak and E. Martin, *Professional Interviewing* (Cambridge: Harper & Row, 1980).

8
HOW CAN YOU PROCESS UNCERTAINTY?

Anything significant is inherently uncertain
and therefore all judgments are probabilistic.
—*Robert Rubin*

The former Secretary of the Treasury, Robert Rubin, along with his friend, Alan Greenspan, helped shape one of the best economies in U.S. history. His sentiments shrewdly capture the mindset of effective leaders. Developing such sensibilities requires intellectual dexterity and determination of the highest order. It requires a special fortitude to endure the inevitable failures while trusting your instincts and pressing on. It requires an ability to weigh options, the willingness to take calculated risks, and the discernment to select the right time to act. The process can start by identifying the misconceptions that many people have nurtured for years. We present the notions below to increase the odds of developing more leaders like Robert Rubin.

Misconceptions

Misconception 1: Postponing a Decision Is a Bad Idea

Sometimes delaying a decision translates into avoiding the inevitable, as with the proverbial ostrich burying its head in the sand.[1] At other times, postponing a decision provides a way to maximize flexibility and attain the optimal solution. Discerning the difference is not always an easy matter. As four-star general Dick Cavazos perceptively observed:

> Most savvy tactical commanders wait until the last minute to decide something. Why is that? Well, that gets back to what you are trying to do. That gets back to this: you want to stay out ahead of the enemy. That means you don't want to decide too far in advance what you're going to do. If you do that, by the time you execute, the situation may have changed, and you may have another option available to you. . . . Well this drives the staff nuts. Why? They've got a lot of details to attend to, so they want the commander to decide very early. . . . So if they don't understand why the commander is doing what he's doing, then they're going to look at their commander as indecisive. In fact, he isn't indecisive at all. What he's looking for is the right intuitive moment to act. Then he executes very forcefully without looking back.[2]

Deferring the decision to the last moment allows leaders to explore many possible options. In a sense, determining when to attack involves discerning the proper balance between exploring the options and refining the battle plan. Sometimes when you delay, you are not like the ostrich but like a hawk surveying a field of prey. Thus, our reconceptualization: Postponing a decision may be a great idea.

Misconception 2: Effective Leaders Focus on Predicting the Future

Sir Winston Churchill may well be one of the greatest leaders of the twentieth century. He summed up his philosophy about the future in the following way: "It is a mistake to look too far ahead, only one link in the chain of destiny can be handled at a time."[3] On another occasion he said: "It is only with some difficulty and within limits that provision can be made for the future. Experience shows that forecasts are usually falsified and preparations always in arrears."[4] One admirer wrote, "Churchill had a rare ability to discern immediately what changes were implied by new facts, and how policy should be adapted to meet the new environment."[5] Therefore, our reconceptualization: Effective leaders are wary of looking too far ahead.

Misconception 3: Order Always Creates Understanding

In fact, the way people organize information may provide comfort but actually inhibit deeper insight. Why? Because most organizational systems direct attention to one or possibly two attributes while ignoring others for the sake of simplicity. For example, a dictionary organizes the words in the language by alphabetical order. What's ignored? The relationship between the words. "Order" and "chaos" are separated by hundreds of pages, yet they help to define one another. To understand these simple relationships and even more complex ones, you need something more than a dictionary. You need a thesaurus, which proves far more valuable to most authors than a dictionary.[6]

In a similar way, a company's financial statement may at once be orderly, neat, and misleading because critical relationships are obscured. Likewise, most restaurant guidebooks tend to be organized by types of cuisine or location, rather than by describing how they fit into a neighborhood.[7] In both cases, experience leads to a deeper and richer knowledge. Thus, our reconceptualization: The existing order may actually inhibit deeper understanding. Table 8.1 summarizes the misconceptions presented in this section.

How Can You Personally Process Uncertainty?

Processing uncertainty requires people to develop a different mind-set. The following ideas suggest how to develop such a perspective on events.

Table 8.1

Common Misconceptions

Misconception	Reconception
Postponing a decision is a bad idea.	Postponing a decision may be a great idea.
Effective leaders focus on predicting the future.	Effective leaders are wary of looking too far ahead.
Order always creates understanding.	The existing order may actually inhibit deeper understanding.

Think Like a Sailor

Sports psychologists tell us that successful athletes build powerful visual images that seep into their unconscious. The images help create robust intuitions informing their right brains of what they find difficult to articulate. We have suggested before that most images (e.g., step of stairs) encourage a certainty mentality. The sailing image has a decidedly different character.

Most people like to get to their destinations quickly and directly. Maybe that's why more people own powerboats than sailboats. Powerboats zip right to their destination, while sailboats zigzag all over to get where they are going. If you watch good sailors, you will notice how they quickly change the position of their sails to take advantage of shifts in the wind. Even though their objective may be directly into the face of the wind, they have to sail at angles; first this way, then that. In fact, zigzagging is the only way to get to their objective. Since the wind shifts, you can't always plan when you will zig and when you will zag. They call this *tacking*. Many people think that sailboats "catch the wind," pushing the vessel along like a wave, but that only happens some of the time. Much of the time you only go forward by arranging the air pressures on the sail in such a way to achieve your objective.

Similarly, effective leaders learn to arrange the pressures in a way that allows them to achieve their objectives. This usually means they have to make some strange zigzags that may even appear to be changes in direction. Their objectives don't change, but how they get there does. Thus, the sailor's mind-set, by necessity, is one that embraces uncertainty. As this image seeps into their unconscious, "setbacks" are transformed into mere shifts in the winds.

Explore Contingencies

It's not always possible to "plan with the end in mind," because you only have a vague sense of the end point. Instead, when there is uncertainty, leaders must "plan" with possibilities in mind. The chess player knows he wants to checkmate the opponent but doesn't know how that will happen until the match starts. In fact, you can't get a clear picture of the endgame until you see what develops. Sports commentators often applaud those teams who "stick with the game plan." What they mean is not always clear. If the game plan is rigid and not working, then sticking with it is an unwise idea. After all, the former Soviet Union mindlessly stuck with the "centralized planning" game plan. On the other hand, if the game plan includes various contingencies, then sticking with the plan assumes an entirely different character.

Scenario-based training focuses attention on the uniqueness of an ever-changing situation. Perhaps this is why officers of the Marine Corps are exposed to hundreds of hours of cases and scenarios in their elite training schools. Their rationale: This is the only way to develop the fundamental pattern-recognition skills necessary to flexibly respond to truly chaotic situations riddled with incomplete and often erroneous information.[8] The scenarios and case studies encourage the troops to see critical relationships, anticipate various courses of action, and discover the core patterns of success.

Leaders need similar skills in the corporate battlefield.

Scenario-based planning could be as simple as preparing two distinct résumés for different types of jobs. Or it could be more elaborate. Contingency planning may involve setting up checkpoints to ascertain the direction of the business environment at given intervals. Ferreting out the specific implications of contingency thinking should prove exciting and illuminating. The hard part is creating the mind-set in the first place.

Avoid Inflexible Commitments to any Single Idea or Solution

Exploring possible contingencies teaches leaders another important skill: when to abandon preexisting notions. Building this kind of mind-set requires a special sort of integrity, especially when you've devoted a lot of energy to a particular idea. Steven Pinker of the Massachusetts Institute of Technology appears to possess this rare quality. Few scientists and even fewer authors would openly acknowledge their fallibility. In the opening pages of his book, *How the Mind Works*, he wrote: "Every idea in the book may turn out to be wrong, but that would be progress, because our old ideas were too vapid to be wrong."[9]

Transferring such sentiments from the scientific to the work-a-day world often proves difficult.[10] The challenge lies in knowing when to switch the game plan. This may be the most elusive competency of all. Two scholars put it this way:

> Executives become so strongly wedded to a particular project, technology, or process that they find themselves continuing when they should pull out. Instead of terminating or redirecting the failing endeavor, managers frequently continue pouring in more resources.[11]

No one knows the magic formula for discerning the time to "cut your losses," but you may want to consider the following ideas:

· Pay attention to the critics; they may be right.
· Provide face-saving alternatives for those who are truly committed to the idea.
· Seek outside independent counsel on the matter.

In short, commitment to problem identification and problem solving should trump the leader's devotion to a particular idea or project.

Draw More Pictures and Diagrams

Pictures and diagrams have a way of releasing intuitions. They may be the first step toward articulating something hidden in the unconscious. They also have a way of highlighting relationships and associations.

In one case, a group of supervisors was asked to draw a picture of the ideal relationship between their department and other departments in the company. This led to a discussion of some novel ideas that never would have surfaced in more traditional discussion techniques. By drawing pictures, even "silly" ideas that would normally be filtered out were brought into the discussion. The pictures had a way of legitimizing uncertainty because no one had to make an argument about how to arrive at the ideal state.

Identify Certainty Levels Associated with Critical Facts

Charting certainty levels provides a useful way to take a more critical look at underlying facts. An author used a clever device to explain the role of microbes in causing disease. Table 8.2 presents the chart that he developed to indicate the various levels of certainty.[12]

Table 8.3 presents another example. Many factors could influence an organization's decision to launch a new venture. No one can be 100 percent sure that a customer base will continue to expand, since that involves accurately pre-

Table 8.2

Role of Microbes in Causing Disease

Proven	Suspected	Possible
Ulcers	Arteriosclerosis, heart disease, and stroke	Various other cancers
Stomach cancer	Alzheimer's	Obesity
Liver cancer	Multiple sclerosis	Schizophrenia
Burkitt's lymphoma	Juvenile diabetes	Manic depression
Cervical cancer	Asthma	Homosexual orientation
Nasopharangeal cancer	Nonmelanoma skin cancer	
Oral cancer	Colon cancer	

dicting the future. By labeling certainty levels, the organization can clearly see the true risks that are inherent to any decision. If the decision turns out to be a poor one, executives can always point to the risky nature of the decision in the first place. This beats the alternatives, such as becoming mired in self-doubt, avoiding future opportunities, or searching for scapegoats. It also creates a specific opportunity to learn from a mistake. For instance, executives may learn that they put too much faith in the findings of marketing studies. All too often executives only think about the known without the context of the unknown. Therefore, charting both the certainties and uncertainties can be helpful in providing more realistic views of an organization's environment.

Enjoy the Ride

Contemplating the possibilities of uncertainty should be invigorating and fun. Successful brainstormers are excited and energized. One of the founders of the wildly successful Yahoo! Internet site described his reactions about developing

Table 8.3

Certainty Levels Associated with New Product Launches

Critical facts	Certainty level (%)
The customer base will continue to expand.	60
No other competitors will enter the market.	60
Economic growth will continue.	85
The market entry price will remain stable.	80
Our revenue stream will continue to increase.	95

the business: "[It's like] being dropped off a helicopter, and you're the first guy skiing down this hill. You don't know where the tree is, you don't know where the cliff is, but it's a great feeling."[13] Thus, successfully processing uncertainty not only requires intellectual skills, but also a more intangible ability to suppress fears, guide emotional energy, and inspire enthusiasm.

How Can You Get Your Organization to Process Uncertainty?

In a word, communicate. Our research unequivocally demonstrated that communication was the key to helping employees to process the implicit uncertainties of organizational life. In fact, when we asked the employees in our database the following open-ended question: "How could your organization make you more comfortable managing uncertainty in the workplace?," well over 50 percent discussed the importance of communication (see Appendix C). Creating greater sensitivity to uncertainty is the easy part. Communicating about the uncertainty often proves more challenging. It means discussing opportunities, perceiving nuances, and playing around with fuzzy ideas. Next we review some of the specific ways to foster this kind of discussion.

Use Methods That Encourage Dialogue Not Monologue

Leaders who foster dialogue encourage give-and-take between employees and allow them to influence the outcome of decisions. Monologue does not. As a result, employees do not have the opportunity to react to the uncertainty in an appropriate way. Processing uncertainty often requires employees to go through the stages of denial, anger, bargaining, depression, and acceptance.[14] This process naturally occurs as ideas and emotions ping from one person to another during dialogue. Figure 8.1 presents some characteristics and examples of dialogue versus monologue.

Often this means deemphasizing formal presentations. In the typical hour-long presentation, only five to ten minutes are devoted to questions. These questions are often perfunctory or merely asking for clarification. Allocating half the allotted time for discussion changes the nature of the questions and allows for alternative viewpoints to be entertained. Or, leaders could decrease the formality of the presentation by allowing more discussion *during* the presentation, instead of at the end. Assumptions can be challenged, critical relationships explored, and core values tested. The objective: Change the nature of presentations from a stereotypical "sales pitch" to a more engaging consideration of possibilities. One critic put it this way, "The more PowerPoint presentations you prepare, the more the world seems to package itself into slide-sized chunks, broken down into bullet items or grouped in geometric patterns that have come to have almost talismanic force."[15] In fact, at one point the Chairman of the Joint Chiefs of Staff, General Hugh Shelton, took on the "PowerPoint Rangers" and issued an order calling for more brevity and sanity in briefings, that is, fewer bells and whistles and more salient information.[16] He, no doubt, recognized that monologue tends to support convention, while dialogue fosters innovation, flexibility, and mental acumen.

Figure 8.1 **Characteristics and Examples of "Dialogue" and "Monologue"**

Dialogue
- Give and take
- Anyone influences outcomes
- Usually face-to-face
- Rich channels (e.g., oral, much feedback)

Examples
- Training sessions
- Strategic planning retreats
- Performance reviews
- Task forces

Monologue
- Less interactive
- Few influence outcomes
- Usually one-to-many
- Lean channels (e.g., written, less feedback)

Examples
- Company newsletter
- Flyers in paychecks
- Intranet
- Direct mail

Explore the Unknown With Others

When a group experiences something new, old roles have a way of changing and interesting dialogue starts to occur.

- One plant manager had his senior staff take a photography class together.
- Another group decided to help build a house through the Habitat for Humanity program.
- A CEO participated in an Outward Bound program with his staff.

In each case the group reported that their relationships had changed; they had more respect for one another's strengths and weaknesses. Interestingly, when asked precisely how their group had changed, they had difficulty finding the right words. Perhaps this is because they merely had a better intuition about how to work together. Or maybe they developed greater confidence in their ability to problem solve. In either case, exploring the unknown with others appears to improve a team's ability to deal with uncertainty.

Consistently Frame Challenges, Not Specific Solutions

A frame provides the lens through which employees view organizational events, highlighting certain attributes of the situation, while deflecting attention from others. When leaders consistently frame uncertainty, they create a viewpoint that implicitly focuses employee energy, helping them make sense of the chaos and confusion. A proper frame allows employees to see the "big picture" amidst the day-to-day complexities. It spotlights the grand challenge, while diverting gaze from specific solutions.

Consider the frame one executive used when his plant decided to change production patterns. In order to remain competitive, the plant had to switch from long runs of a few products to shorter runs of many products. Such a massive transformation required procedural modifications, millions of dollars of new equipment, and, most difficult of all, changes in the employees' mind-set. And they had to absorb all this tumultuous complexity while they continued to produce their traditional product lines. The plant manager decided to frame the situation with a consistent theme during the transition. He explained, "Our challenge is to continue performing while we transform the plant." "Transforming while performing" became the plant mantra for several years. It provided a sense of motivation by legitimizing the efforts of those who kept the old equipment "performing" while others installed the new "transforming" machines. It also helped make sense of confusing events like using resources to purchase new equipment instead of upgrading existing machines. In fact, despite all the change, production levels continued to rise during this time period.

This frame was effective for a number of reasons. The words rhyme. They are simple. And they are easy to remember. The use of verbs directs attention to action, both in the present and the future. But "transforming while performing" was more than a clever slogan. Most importantly, the frame addressed a deep underlying organizational issue that resonated with employees and focused attention on the plant's future.

Discuss Different Models of the Situation

Such discussions have a way of generating dialogue based on different perspectives. Why? Because models use different assumptions. Consequently, they provide various explanations and yield unique predictions. At the very least, debating those differences creates an awareness of viable alternatives. Most individuals make appropriate as well as inappropriate assumptions that lie hidden beyond their awareness. Ridding an organization of inappropriate but latent assumptions presents leaders with a devilish problem. It resembles the challenge of separating salt from seawater but can prove as life-altering as a cold drink for a thirsty survivor. But once the assumptions are identified, they can be easily discarded. Over time as some assumptions prove more appropriate than others, some responses become more appropriate than others.

Figure 8.2 vividly addresses a chaotic and uncertain situation: Where will the hurricane hit land? Answer: At the time no one knew or could have known. What to do? Examine different models of the situation based on different assumptions. In time, one set of assumptions proved more appropriate. The power of the map lies in legitimizing various alternatives while underscoring the importance of monitoring the situation. Any organization could engage in meaningful discussion using a similar approach. After all, the business climate changes almost as frequently as the weather.

Focus the Communication System on Thinking Routines and Speed

Traditionally, organizations have treated communication as a highly scripted affair based on formal quarterly meetings and monthly newsletters. The messages focus almost exclusively on *what* the company *knows* rather than *how it thinks* about issues. There is another, more effective alternative.

By reorienting the communication system, we assisted one paper manufacturer in encouraging its 1,000 employees to more readily embrace uncertainty.[17] We did this by first introducing a biweekly "pulse" survey that systematically questioned a random group of employees about several key plant issues. For instance, employees were asked to respond to the question, "If you could ask the plant manager one question, what would it be?" We then issued a report, the Pulse Report, which summarized several key issues that emerged from the survey.[18] Supervisors in the plant were

Figure 8.2   **Mapping Uncertainty**

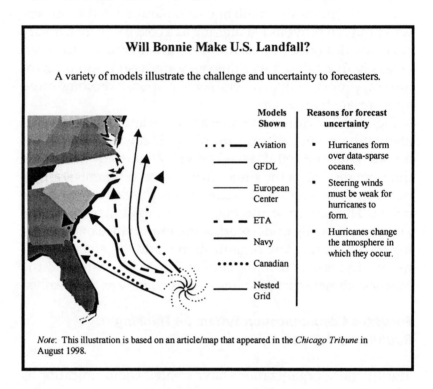

Will Bonnie Make U.S. Landfall?

A variety of models illustrate the challenge and uncertainty to forecasters.

Models Shown	Reasons for forecast uncertainty
· · · — Aviation	▪ Hurricanes form over data-sparse oceans.
——— GFDL	
——— European Center	▪ Steering winds must be weak for hurricanes to form.
▪ — — ETA	
——— Navy	▪ Hurricanes change the atmosphere in which they occur.
· · · · · · Canadian	
——— Nested Grid	

Note: This illustration is based on an article/map that appeared in the *Chicago Tribune* in August 1998.

briefed on the report and they, in turn, were expected to update their employees. A separate "Talking Points" document was prepared for the supervisors, which served as the basis for their discussions with their crews (see Table 8.4). The standard format of the document contained four basic pieces of information:

· the key issues;
· a story or learning opportunity;
· what the company knows *now* about the issue; and
· what the company *does not* know *now* about the issue.

Table 8.4

Manager Talking Points

Issue	Story/learning opportunity	What do we know *now*?	What do we *not* know now?
Communication	As times change, so must the communication system. In the old days, most folks expected to wait for a full and complete news report from the newspaper. Nowadays, we get instant news that is partial and incomplete. Then we piece together the picture. In a sense, we need to make the same transition and learn to appropriately respond to partial information.	The difficulty of communicating during times of rapid change is that predictions and plans about the future are constantly in flux. We are meeting the challenge by communicating more frequently and through a variety of channels such as weekly manager briefings and the newsletter.	Unclear: How long it will take employees to move from an expectation of "complete" information to a reliance on a more rapid communication system.
		A number of retiring employees have remarked in exit interviews that they have seen improvement in communication practices over the years.	Unknown: How long it will take all employees to improve their communication skills.
		Over the last six months, the Pulse Report has shown a steady improvement in the number of employees who report that they "understand where the company is headed."	
Long-term job security	The best way to ensure job security is to:	We are doing well on both efforts (costs and new products).	Unknown: With any new products, some will fail, and some will succeed. While initial tests show positive customer response, we don't know which products will be successful. But, that is all part of the challenge of adapting to the needs of an ever-changing marketplace.
	1. reduce costs.	We are introducing four new products this quarter.	
	2. vigorously pursue new products that meet customer needs.	We are testing out new marketing techniques, such as hiring a telemarketing firm to sell certain products.	Unknown: We are hopeful about the telemarketing effort, but we don't know how it will work out.

What did this achieve? We used the Pulse Report to increase the *speed and focus* of communication efforts. Checking the "pulse" of the plant and issuing employees a rapid response addressed issues as they emerged rather than unveiling them in the biannual climate survey. Also, the "story" or learning opportunity tapped in to how management thought about these issues, in essence their "thinking routines." Unlike most information, the "thinking routines" tended to endure, providing employees with a greater sense of stability. Initially, employees were shocked to see management admit that there were things they did *not* know. Over time, though, the employees developed trust in the communication system, realizing that partial, but fast information could provide the necessary degree of comfort. In short, we discovered that speed trumped completeness. In fact, as a result of the Pulse Report, Talking Points, and related communications, the percentage of employees who reported they "understood the direction of the plant" increased from 30 to 80 percent over a two-year period.

Conclusion

International Business Machine's lead counsel once said, "We buy from competitors. We sell to the same competitors. We sue competitors. We've got complex relationships."[19] If executives are mired in such complexity, then employees must be even more confused. Yet, IBM is still one of the most admired and profitable businesses in the world. This is exactly the kind of environment most organizations, large and small, must learn to master. They do so by embracing, not ignoring, the uncertainty. Employees, even those who desire stability, recognize the necessity of thriving in an uncertain environment. Learning how to discern the possibilities, make decisions, and communicate in a probabilistic world, not in an artificially certain one, is the only way that leaders can, in Robert Rubin's words, accomplish "anything significant."

Notes

1. Ostriches don't really bury their heads in the sand. Ostriches often lie flat on the ground to escape detection. This practice may have given rise to the legend.

2. T. Clancy, *Into the Storm: A Study of Command* (New York: G.P. Putnam, 1997), p. 101.

3. M. Gilbert, *Churchill: A Life* (New York: Henry Holt, 1991), p. 827.

4. M. Gilbert, *Winston S. Churchill*, vol. 7 (London: Heinemann, 1971), p. 12.

5. S. Hayward, *Churchill on Leadership: Executive Success in the Face of Adversity* (Rocklin, CA: Prima, 1997), p. 89.

6. There actually two kinds of thesauruses; one is organized alphabetically, the other by concepts. Clearly we prefer the later one!

7. R. Wurman, "Redesign the Data," *Business 2.0*, 28 November 2000, 210–220.

8. D. Freedman, "Corps Values," *Inc.* April 1998, 56–65.

9. S. Pinker, *How the Mind Works* (New York: W.W. Norton, 1997), p. ix.

10. J. Kruger and D. Dunning, "Unskilled and Unaware of It: How Difficulties in Recognizing One's Own Incompetence Lead to Inflated Self-Assessments," *Journal of Personality and Social Psychology* 77, no. 6 (1999): 1121–1134.

11. M. Keil and R. Montealegre, "Cutting Your Losses: Extricating Your Organization When a Big Project Goes Awry," *Sloan Management Review* 41, no. 3 (2000): 55–68.

12. P.E. Ross, "Do Germs Cause Cancer?" *Forbes*, 15 November 1999, 194–200.

13. R.H. Reid, *Architects of the Web: 1,000 Days That Built the Future of Business.* (New York: John Wiley, 1997), p. 278.

14. P.G. Clampitt, *Communicating for Managerial Effectiveness* (Thousand Oaks, CA: Sage, 2001).

15. G. Nunberg, "The Trouble with Powerpoint," *Fortune*, 20 December 1999, p. 330–331. Also see Lincoln's Gettysburg address on Powerpoint at www.norvig.com for a vivid and humorous illustration of this notion.

16. G. Jaffe, "What's Your Point, Lieutenant? Just Cut to the Pie Charts," *Wall Street Journal*, 26 April 2000, A1, 13.

17. P. G. Clampitt, B. DeKoch, and T. Cashman, "A Strategy for Communicating About Uncertainty," *Academy of Management Executive* 14, no. 4 (2000): 41–57.

18. Ibid. See also O. Hargie and D. Tourish, *Handbook of Communication Audits For Organisations*, (London: Routledge, 2000).

19. B. Morris, "Big Blue," *Fortune*, 14 April 1997, 68–81.

9
HOW CAN YOU CATALYZE ACTION DURING UNCERTAIN TIMES?

Simple rules are adopted by people who
acknowledge [the] possibility of error up front, and then
seek to minimize it in practice. Complex rules are for
those who have an unattainable vision of perfection.
—*Richard A. Epstein*

His accomplishments spanned a dazzling array of disciplines. He struck out on his own at the age of seventeen, starting a printing shop that provided him financial security for the rest of his life. He was an innovator, creating a new stove that furnished more heat with less fuel. He was a civic leader, organizing the first fire company in Philadelphia and the first public library in the United States. He was a political leader as well, helping draft the Declaration of Independence and serving as a skilled diplomat for his country. He was also a famous scientist, dramatically demonstrating that lightning is an electrical phenomenon. One of his biographers made this observation:

> Many people find uncertainty unsettling and insist on definite answers to the large and small questions of life. [He] was just the opposite, being of that less numerous tribe that finds certainty—or certitude, rather—unsettling. [His approach] reflected his wide, and ever widening, reading, which exposed him to multiple viewpoints. Above all, it probably reflected something

innate . . . he contented himself with incomplete answers, maintaining an open mind and seeming to skate upon life's surface.[1]

"Poor Richard" never directly discussed how to catalyze action during uncertain times, but his temperament wonderfully symbolizes the ideas discussed in this chapter.

Misconceptions

Leaders like Benjamin Franklin possess a remarkable ability to distinguish myth from reality, thus providing the preliminary conditions for catalyzing action. We discuss the most debilitating of these myths in this section.

Misconception 1: You Can't Go Forward Until You Know Everything

The information age was supposed to free leaders to make better decisions. In fact, it may bury them in reports, studies, and e-mail. It confronts leaders with a dilemma: Namely, will more information help? Sometimes it will. At other times, waiting for more information produces paralysis driven by a false belief that you can't do anything until you know everything. Therefore, our reconceptualization: Progress usually requires making decisions based on incomplete information.

Misconception 2: Any Decision Is Better Than Indecision

This myth lies on the flip side of the first one. The CEO of Disney, Michael Eisner, made this insightful comment:

> Sometimes an instant "I love it. Let's go make it now" response is appropriate. But more often, some delay helps. Now, we've been accused of not giving quick answers . . . if delay is a tactic to test someone's passion for an idea, to incubate it, whether it be an actor or director or another executive, then delay is good.[2]

Discerning when to delay action for thoughtful reflection and when to push ahead for meaningful experimentation may well be the quintessential leadership skill during times of uncertainty. Therefore, our reconceptualization: The best decision may involve practicing strategic patience.

Misconception 3: Every Step Must Be a Step Forward

A staircase is nice, neat, and linear. It is also precisely the wrong image for exploring unknown territory. There are not many staircases in the Rocky Mountains. In fact, rock climbers zigzag all over the face of the mountain to reach the summit. There is no direct path. By the time Kitty Calhoun turned thirty, she already scaled two of the highest mountains on the planet.[3] The world-class climber explained her philosophy of climbing: "You have to be patient, determined, and focused. Like playing a game of chess, you change strategy all the time."[4] She expects obstacles and detours. When the climber backs down, she has a new vantage point from which to view the situation. She may have learned something in the course of her ascent that she had not anticipated. Then she adjusts her plans. The pattern is:

- assess the situation;
- climb;
- reassess the situation;
- climb;
- repeat as often as necessary.

Each assessment is like a platform from which she can decide if her current plans can be executed, or other options need to be explored. Who gets motivated to constantly reassess when climbing a staircase? It's difficult to do so; you are stuck with one path. Yet, those who embrace uncertainty are always thinking of the alternate path. The summit constantly beckons, but plans are often changing. Thus, our reconceptualization: Discovering the alternative path may be the only way to move forward.

How Can You Personally Catalyze Action?

Dispelling myths helps create the right conditions (see Table 9.1), but leaders need effective strategies as well. We review the most important ones in this section.

Look for the Deeper Pattern

Often times the only way to deal with complexity is to look for a deeper pattern. For instance, making accurate weather forecasts is notoriously difficult. There are a host of factors to consider: wind speed, wind direction, moisture, temperature, and atmospheric pressure, to name a few. Then, of course, all these factors interact, making the task of prediction even more daunting. Yet, despite the many improvements in technologies and mathematical models, the accuracy of a typical five-day forecast did not significantly improve until the discovery of jet streams. Meteorologists soon learned that the position of a jet stream was a pivotal factor that influenced temperatures, wind directions, and humidity levels. The discovery of the deeper pattern provided a viable way to understand the immense complexity of our local weather.

Likewise, prescient businesses look for deeper patterns in their environments. For instance, executives at several leading breweries in the United States are quietly seeking ways to avoid the same calamities experienced by tobacco companies.[5] They have discerned a pattern that begins with warning labels and ends in debilitating lawsuits. Presumably thinking about such issues now can provide these companies with more viable options in the future. Even though they don't know exactly what may happen, they can at least

Table 9.1

Common Misconceptions

Misconception	Reconception
You can't go forward until you know everything.	Progress usually requires making decisions based on incomplete information.
Any decision is better than indecision.	The best decision may involve practicing strategic patience.
Every step must be a step forward.	Discovering the alternative path may be the only way to step forward.

set in motion policies designed to either avoid the lawsuits altogether or limit future liabilities. That beats the alternative of being surprised.

Experiment

Experiments are a useful alternative when faced with complexity or the unknown. The chances are good that the company can learn something and happen on a useful principle or rule of thumb. For example, for years Appleton Papers has been a dominant force in the carbonless paper market. Consumers use this kind of paper whenever they sign their credit card receipt or fill out a multi-part form. But the company recognized that because of the greater use of computer technology, the carbonless market is on a slow but definite downward trend. Consequently, they developed the "GO" (Growth Opportunities) process, which is designed to find an array of new products that the company could produce that exploits their unique knowledge and capabilities to coat paper. Some of the product ideas proved unsuccessful; others are emerging as profit centers. But they expected this and used the experimental "failures" to hone their marketing and production skills.

Experiments need not be conducted on such a grand scale.

A minor league hockey team, the Utah Grizzlies, toyed with idea of purchasing a high-speed digital color copier to print up brochures, posters, and other promotional items. At first blush the idea seemed like a pleasant convenience, allowing the staff to avoid the hassle of outsourcing arrangements. They decided to try out several of these machines on a trial basis. The experimental results: Not only did the machine make life easier for employees, but the company discovered a new way to increase customer satisfaction and profitability.[6] In short, experiments on a large or small scale allow companies to continually reproduce their success on many levels.

Play the Odds

In some cases, randomness has a pattern that allows some level of prediction. Professional oddsmakers do a pretty good job. Even though they are often wrong with their individual predictions, over time they are pretty close to the mark. After all, in the long run the casino wins. So if organizations can ascertain the general odds in an uncertain situation, it would be wise to play them. For instance, general managers of professional football teams routinely make personnel decisions on this basis. They may not know *who* will be injured, but they make decisions about the number of backups based on *the odds* of injuries. Few teams carry backup punters.

Likewise, businesses cannot expect every marketing initiative to pay off. For instance, Rockwell Automation has used traditional marketing distribution channels for many years. Recently, they made a major investment in another approach based on an e-commerce model while augmenting their traditional distribution channels by investing in electronic automation. Julie Sadoff, manager of e-business communication explains, "We've hedged our bet by investing in both the traditional system and e-commerce. This dual investment strategy distinguishes us from our competitors."[7] Given the underlying nature of B2B commerce, the odds are that one or both approaches will pay off.

Sometimes, though, you have to make a choice. When faced with randomness, your best course may be to figuratively "flip the coin." Or you can ask the bunny. That's exactly what Norm Brodsky did when his company faced a tough decision about making a correct bid on a million-dollar contract. After careful research, his advisors simply couldn't decide on which bid to submit. If they bid too high, they would lose the contract. If they bid too low, they might unnecessarily lower their margins. What to do? The company happened to have an office pet with a taste for M&M's.® So the management team wrote out each bid on a separate piece of paper. Then they strategically placed an M&M on top of each slip of paper and placed the slips in separate corners of the room. The bunny was released from the cage. He sniffed one of the treats but hopped away to another side of the room and ate that one. The slip of paper under that M&M became the company's bid; it turned out to be exactly the right bid to get the contract and preserve the margins. As Norm reminds us, it was not just "dumb luck" because a lot of effort went into researching the bids. Yet he also recognized that, "Business is not a completely rational process. There are always factors beyond your control—some that you're aware of, some that hit you out of the blue."[8]

Don't Ignore Your Intuitions

One of your authors was asked by a local television station to critique the Bush–Gore Presidential Debates. Anxieties started popping up like dandelions on a hot summer day: How will I look? Will I say something inappropriate? But if you are writing a book on embracing uncertainty, you get out the weed-eater and go face the klieg lights. The news anchors always wanted to know who "won" the debate. The question is more complex than it appears and really can't be answered until days after the event. It involves anticipating the responses of millions of citizens as they debate what they saw and heard, not only from the candidates, but also from friends, colleagues, and pundits. What to do? When facing situations demanding quick responses to complex questions, experts learn to rely on their intuitions. And that is exactly what your coauthor did, predicting that prior expectations of the candidates would significantly impact the public's view of the "winner."

In fact, one study of managers found that two-thirds of them felt that using intuition led to better decisions.[9] Intuition expedites decision making, promotes the synthesis of information, and provides a check on data-driven analyses. Some have called the reliance on intuition irrational. (But what about irrational numbers? There was a time when they were not accepted by the mathematical community. Now rational and irrational numbers are collectively known as real numbers. Perhaps there is a lesson here.) A cautionary note: We are not talking about some kind of whimsical hunch that provides a convenient excuse to avoid contradictory evidence.[10] Intuition works best when grounded in experience; clearly the intuition of an expert is more reliable than that of a nonexpert. That's why effective leaders hone their intuitions by looking for the deeper pattern, experimenting, and playing the odds.

Assess the Type and Degree of Uncertainty

We have suggested that there are at least three factors that can create uncertainty: ignorance, randomness, and complexity (see Chapter 3). Clearly, many situations, such as a crisis, contain elements of all three. However, it is important to recognize that each type may need special treatment. For instance, while more information can help solve a problem of ignorance, it is useless in the face of randomness. Moreover, the degree of uncertainty varies from situation to situation. This can also alter your response. If there is a fork in the road, you can clearly plan for either path. But what if there aren't any roads? Then, of course, you will have to rely on something even more fundamental than a plan. You will have to rely on your intuition and your ability to reason and recognize patterns. Table 9.2 can help you sort through your options.

How Can You Get Your Organization to Catalyze Action During Uncertain Times?

Leaders who can spur others to appropriate action during uncertainty provide their organizations with a unique competitive advantage. But doing so requires special talents and a unique orientation. The ideas reviewed in this section are designed to build those competencies.

Hire the Right People

Recently researchers have coined terms like "emotional intelligence" or the "adversity quotient" to explain the differences between successful and unsuccessful employees. The researchers have concluded that even very intelligent people can fail because they lack these qualities.[11] Regardless of the label, *the more fundamental quality* of *successful people appears to be the ability to act in the face of uncertainty.* "Emotionally intelligent" people can work with others to reach a consensus solution that satisfies most if not all of their aims. People with a high "adversity quotient" can overcome the inevitable setbacks associated with attempting new tasks. One company executive, focusing on becoming an innovative leader, put it this way: "We used to hire people who were great at implementing our long-term plans. Now our long-term plan lasts about a quarter. We've got two alternatives: Either change the thinking of the people we have or hire people who think differently. And, frankly, I don't think we'll be able to transform our implementers into innovators."[12]

Smash the Clock

Often it takes time for an innovative idea to find its niche. Brandon Tartikoff, the late programming genius at NBC, stuck with innovative concept shows like *Hill Street Blues,*

Table 9.2

Assessing the Type of Uncertainty

Type of uncertainty	Signs	Examples	Proper responses	Improper responses
Ignorance	Information is limited	The first stage of a crisis	Conduct further research	Force an answer
	No one has tried to answer questions like these before	Trying to discover or create something	Make plausible assumptions	Stick to the "game plan"
	Projections into the future	"What-if" questions or unknowable answers	Experiment	
	Response to questions is based on conjecture or "gut feelings"		Explore the unknown	
Randomness	Attempts at specific prediction prove useless	The roll of the dice	Play the odds	Conduct further research
	Fluctuations reveal no underlying pattern	Determining where lightning is going to strike	See what happens, then react	Force an answer
Complexity	Confusion	War	Postpone the decision	Flip a coin
	Information overload	The tax code	Experiment	Stick to the "game plan"
	Changing one variable changes a number of others	An ecosystem	Look for deeper level patterns	
	Many levels of a system at work simultaneously	A computer network	See what happens, then react	
	Many perspectives and points of view	A bureaucracy		

Cheers, and *L.A. Law* even when they languished in the ratings during their initial seasons. Other executives would have axed them after much shorter trials. Sometimes the wisest decision is to delay the decision. In fact, pushing deadlines at all costs can lead to a fire-fighting mentality in organizations. In *Harvard Business Review,* one scholar explained:

> Instead, be flexible about deadlines. Measure development projects by the number of outstanding problems. Most companies measure "open issues" and problems discovered after product release, and many good factories have accurate lists and measures of unsolved problems. If this list stays the same or grows for more than a month after a product introduction, the organization is in fire-fighting mode.[13]

In short, the deadline may not cause the fires, but it can fan the flames. And few leaders, even as skilled as Tartikoff, can creatively embrace uncertainty while crises blaze through the organization.

"Smashing the clock" has other benefits as well. Some issues of great complexity take a great deal of time to really understand. Scheduling several rounds of discussion on the same topic can be helpful. Sometimes by "sleeping on an idea," an unconscious reconciliation of conflicting ideas can emerge. One of Microsoft's secrets to success is that while their product development timetables are often aggressive, they still build a lot of flexibility into their processes. They routinely allocate 20–50 percent of the schedule to unforeseen changes, improvements, and developments. Consequently, product features evolve over time. "The final feature list may change and grow 20–30 percent, depending on how work proceeds, what competitors do, or what type of feedback the project members get during development."[14] Executives not only acknowledge this fact of high tech life, they embrace it. In fact, without this intrinsic adaptability, the fortunes of these companies can literally vanish with the click of a mouse.

Delaying decision making can also provide more flexibility in meeting challenges.[15] Consider the pressure that Leonardo daVinci was under when painting the "Last Supper." His patron was astonished by his lack of progress on the painting. Yet every brush stroke was completed except the face of one disciple. For months he delayed painting the last face. When pressed on the issue, he replied that he had been working on it for two hours every day. But the Duke could not understand how the artist could work on a painting he had not seen in months. Leonardo responded:

> Your Excellency is aware that only the head of Judas remains to be done, and he was, as everyone knows, an egregious villain. Therefore he should be given a physiognomy fitting his wickedness. To this end, for about a year if not more, night and morning, I have been going every day to the Borghetto, where Your Excellency knows that all the ruffians of the city live. But I have not yet been able to discover a villain's face corresponding to what I have in mind. Once I find that face, I will finish the painting in a day.[16]

He goes on to suggest that if his efforts proved fruitless, he would use the face of the person who complained to the Duke in the first place. His Excellency was pleased with the great artist's explanation. The pressure ceased, and the masterpiece was completed. These are not the mere musings of an eccentric artist; they are, in fact, the sentiments of one who recognized the artistic element in all kinds of endeavors. After all, Leonardo was also a skilled architect, inventor, scientist, and engineer.

Foster "Focused Flexibility"

In the Book of Proverbs, King Solomon admonishes, "Go to the ant, you lazybones; consider its ways, and be wise" (Proverbs 6:6). It's not just the ant's work ethic; it is the way they work together that proves illuminating. Some scientists call it "swarm smarts" or "swarm intelligence."[17] It emerges from their collective behavior, allowing them to solve complex logistics issues like finding the shortest distance to good food sources. As two scientists observed, "By maintaining pheromone trails and continuously exploring new paths, the ants serendipitously set up a backup plan and thus are prepared to respond to changes in their environment."[18] Ants have a remarkable ability to quickly forget old pathways and switch roles as needs of the swarm change. In other words, ants practice "focused flexibility"; they *focus* on present needs while maintaining the *flexibility* to meet future ones.

Some companies are now beginning to recognize the wisdom of such an approach when responding to environmental uncertainty. Two strategy scholars observed:

> Managers of [successful] companies know that the greatest opportunities for competitive advantage lie in market confusion, so they jump into chaotic markets, probe for opportunities, build on successful forays, and shift flexibly among opportunities as circumstances dictate. But they recognize the need for a few key strategic processes and a few simple rules to guide them through the chaos.[19]

Sounds just like the ants! Focus provides the motivation, resources, and direction needed to accomplish ever-changing goals. Flexibility allows companies to more quickly respond to marketplace changes while decreasing development costs. On average, designers who use flexible strategies can complete their projects in half the time of those using more conventional design processes.[20]

Maintaining both focus and flexibility tests the leadership abilities of even the most skilled executives. It means developing an ability to quickly inspire others to shift focus with little loss in productivity. It means redefining "the problem from one of improving forecasting to one of eliminating the need for accurate long-term forecasts."[21] It means teaching employees to partially forget the old ways of doing things while maintaining those memories in case they are needed in the future. Above all, it means artfully reconciling the trade-offs between focus and flexibility. Too much focus destroys your flexibility, while too much flexibility crushes your capacity for focus. This is the wisdom gleaned from pondering the ways of the ant.

Develop an Integrated Strategy

No single idea we've discussed can provide the appropriate response to an uncertain situation. Leaders will have to assimilate multiple approaches in order to develop a viable strategy. They acknowledge the uncontrollable but focus on the controllable aspects of the situation.

Consider the approach a group of medical specialists used when faced with growing uncertainty. For years, they maintained offices in the city's two major hospitals. Their clinic was thriving from word-of-mouth referrals by patients to their family and friends. But the 1980s changed all that with the growth and power of health maintenance organizations (HMOs). The doctors discerned a new pattern emerging in the marketplace: Patients would now need a referral from their primary doctor to see these specialists rather than have the freedom of choice they had under traditional insurance plans. The group recognized that referring physicians would exert greater influence on patients' choices of specialists, and in effect, these referring physicians were becoming the "customers." This change in referring patterns produced a lot of uncertainty at the clinic.

The executive team recognized that despite all the changes in the business environment, the fundamental issue was how to form better relationships with referring physicians. If those relationships could be further developed, then the clinic could continue to thrive and expand in this changing health care environment. Sensing this underlying trend proved helpful, but no one knew exactly what to do. So they *focused* their *attention* on this issue. They developed *flexibility* by *experimenting* with a number of ideas, *"playing the odds"* that one or two would prove particularly effective. Meanwhile, they *delayed* the final *decision* until they developed a deeper understanding of the business climate.

One idea involved establishing other satellite offices strategically located around primary care physicians and staffing them on a part-time basis. In the past they would not have considered such an option. But over time the satellite offices became an important tool in forming relationships with the referring physicians. Currently, they are hiring new physicians to staff an ever-growing number of satellite offices. Ironically, now the executive team views the strategy as relative straightforward and inevitable. But during the initial discussions about the uncertainties in the medical field, the path forward was not at all clear. In fact, there was a great deal of hesitation to do anything. But by selectively experimenting, the executive team allowed a viable integrated strategy to emerge.

Concluding Thoughts

The competencies associated with embracing uncertainty require constant practice. Consider the training of the U.S. Air Force's Air Para-Rescue Units (PJs) whose mission involves extracting pilots from hostile territory. As members of Special Operations, these teams are the "elite of the elite" and are trained to handle virtually any medical situation in almost any circumstance, ranging from perilous mountain ranges to violent seas. Learning to professionally face life and death situations under such tenuous conditions is a daunting task. How do they do it? They relentlessly train in a wide range of circumstances: snow, heat, and water. But no matter how rigorous, the training regimen could not possibly include all the potential situations a unit could encounter. *They develop a unique confidence NOT from knowing all the answers ahead of time, but from their ability to creatively and quickly solve problems.* One officer explained it this way: "We've been put in so many 'what if' situations that I know I'll find a way out."[22] He explained that his team might be dropped into a treacherous mountain range for a mission and then asked to perform their task under a variety of conditions such as:

· What if we had no air support?
· What if our food supply runs out?
· What if our communication equipment malfunctions?

By routinely dealing with uncertainty, his team develops an enormous capacity to think of innovative solutions. In short, his team embraces uncertainty by *cultivating awareness* of the possible situations, *processing* them, and then *catalyzing* decisive *action*. Despite the low pay and hazardous duty, the Navy creates a dynamic climate that PJs find motivating, satisfying, and meaningful. Such are the rewards of embracing uncertainty.

Notes

1. H.W. Brands, *The First American: The Life and Times of Benjamin Franklin* (New York: Doubleday, 2000), p. 113. Benjamin Franklin's mind-set may be best captured in his famous maxim, ". . . in this world nothing can be said to be certain, except death and taxes." See Brands, p. 706.

2. Michael Eisner as cited in S. Wetlaufer, "Common Sense and Conflict: An Interview with Disney's Michael Eisner," *Harvard Business Review* 78 no. 1 (2000): 115–124.

3. J. Krakauer, "What's a Nice Southern Girl Doing in a Place Like This?" *Outside Magazine*, June 1993, 60–64.

4. G. Child, "The Frozen Face of Thalay Sagar," *National Geographic*, August 1997, 44–53.

5. Dr. T. Meyer, interview with P. Clampitt, 8 July 2000.

6. M. Lee and J. H. Maxwell, "Local Color," *Inc. Tech* no. 4 (2000): 151–157.

7. J. Sadoff, interview with P. Clampitt, 4 March 2000.

8. N. Brodsky, "Improving Your Luck," *Inc.*, April 1997, 35–36.

9. L.A. Burke and M.K. Miller, "Taking the Mystery Out of Intuitive Decision Making," *Academy of Management Executive* 13, no. 4 (1999): 91–99.

10. W. Agor, *Intuition in Organizations* (Newbury Park, CA: Sage, 1989).

11. D. Goleman, *Emotional Intelligence* (New York: Bantam Books, 1997). Also see P. Stolz, *Adversity Quotient: Turning Obstacles into Opportunities* (New York: John Wiley, 1999).

12. Interview with P. Clampitt, 4 April 2000, source wishes to remain anonymous.

13. R. Bohn, "Stop Fighting Fires," *Harvard Business Review* 78, no. 4 (2000): 83–91.

14. M.A. Cusumano, "How Microsoft Makes Large Teams Work Like Small Teams," *Sloan Management Review* 39, no. 1 (1997): 9–20.

15. T. Clancy, *Into the Storm: A Study in Command* (New York: G. P. Putnam, 1997).

16. S. Bramly, *Leonardo: Discovering the Life of Leonardo da Vinci,* trans. Sian Reynolds (New York: Edward Burlingame Books, 1991), p. 295.

17. E. Bonabeau and G. Théraulaz, "Swarm Smarts," *Scientific American*, March 2000, 73–79.

18. Ibid., 76.

19. K.M. Eisenhardt and D.N. Sull, "Strategy as Simple Rules," *Harvard Business Review* 79, no. 1 (2001): 106–119.

20. S. Thomke and D. Reinertsen, "Agile Product Development: Managing Development Flexibility in Uncertain Environments," *California Management Review* 41, no. 1 (1998): 8–30.

21. Ibid., 11.

22. Captain R. Giacchino, interview with P. Clampitt, 10 January 2000.

10
DOES "EMBRACING UNCERTAINTY" REALLY WORK?

True genius resides in the capacity for evaluation of uncertain, hazardous, and conflicting information.
—Sir Winston Churchill

Anyone can easily misunderstand the embracing uncertainty idea. Those people deeply committed to the certainty culture may *need* to misunderstand. They can then easily dismiss our notions. We have tried to be careful about not overstating our case. Nevertheless, some people may either intentionally or unintentionally get the wrong impression. Therefore, we conclude with a chapter devoted to responses to frequently asked questions.

Personal Application Issues

Question: You were pretty rough on the "know-it-alls." Isn't it a fact that some people know a whole lot more than others?

Response: Yes, there are often great differences among people. But the know-it-all's knowledge shrinks into insignificance when compared to the vast universe of unknowns.

Consider the implications of Figure 10.1. Note the expanse of the universe of the unknown when compared to the region of the known. You might also recognize that the diagram does not even include the larger universe of things that are simply unknowable.

Question: If I embrace uncertainty, won't I appear indecisive?

Response: Someone who embraces uncertainty does not avoid decision making. He or she may put off a decision until the last moment or a more opportune time. This may be *perceived* as indecisive. One way to correct this impression is to clearly communicate your motives: "We need to postpone this decision. I think we need to put more thought into the situation." You are still making progress when you shape the line of inquiry in this manner. Another way to manage the issue is to consider the alternatives. Would you rather appear indecisive, or impulsive and reckless?

Question: Can't people use my uncertainty against me?

Response: Only if you let them. In one sense this book is about shame. You should not be ashamed to say, "I don't know." Everyone lives in a vast ocean of uncertainty, and people construct their little islands of certainty. Those who should be humiliated are those who act as if their island is a kingdom while ignoring the vast unknown beyond. They will, of course, ultimately be swept away by a raging storm of complexity.

Question: Isn't it just natural to try to reduce uncertainty?

Figure 10.1   **Universe of Knowledge**

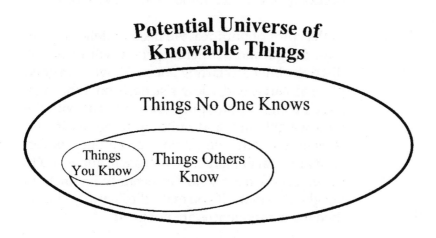

Potential Universe of Knowable Things

Things No One Knows

Things You Know   Things Others Know

Response: Not necessarily. Social scientists, attempting to understand our interpersonal relationships, proposed the "Uncertainty Reduction Theory." The basic idea is simple: When people meet, they use a variety of methods to reduce the uncertainty. For instance, by asking people what they do for a living, you can categorize them and thus know what to talk about with them. Scholars who have studied the theory have concluded that there are some flaws in this basic premise. For instance, one study concluded that "one's tolerance for uncertainty is the critical determinant of information seeking behavior, not one's level of uncertainty."[1] Translation: People have different tolerances for uncertainty. What we are advocating is that leaders need to increase their tolerance level; otherwise, they are living in a fantasy world built by the certainty providers.

Question: You have convinced me. You have a lot of suggestions, but what should be my first step?

Response: In the spirit of our idea, we need to delicately answer this question. Different people will, no doubt, discover different starting points. However, a good place to start is with a low-risk decision. When you start a weight-lifting program, you start with the light weights first and build up to more difficult ones. In the same way, if you can embrace uncertainty in a small matter, then this will allow you to develop and trust your uncertainty instincts in weightier matters. If you make the "wrong" choice, then the consequences are not great.

Work-Related Issues

Question: I understand how I can embrace uncertainty. I even understand how I can get my work group to do it. But what if my boss is not supportive?

Response: An indirect approach might work. You could look for the opportunity to say: "How sure are we of those facts or projections?" This seemingly naïve question opens an epistemological floodgate. It calls into question the entire decision-making and prediction process. In one case, a company's CFO had a penchant for certainty. As a team of executives wrestled with a complex issue, a consultant adroitly introduced this question. A lightbulb went off in the CFO's head; his view of the world was completely transformed. He had to admit that many of the projections were based on assumptions that were, at best, good hunches. He even started preaching the idea of being tolerant of uncertainty to his staff.

Question: If you were only to do one thing in my organization to create an uncertainty-tolerant culture, what
would it be?

Response: Create an awareness of the inherent uncertainty
in decision making. Once you acknowledge uncertainty, you've broken the spell. This will be
debilitating to some, but others will eagerly join
in the process of creatively using the uncertainty.

Question: What about the inevitable stress and tension associated with this approach?

Response: Leaders can encounter stress or tension at either
end of the uncertainty continuum. The question
is "What is more tolerable?" Embracing uncertainty means releasing the stress and tension of
always looking for the "one right answer." Think
of the needless anxiety of searching for the right
answer, only to find there isn't one or that there
are many reasonable answers.

Question: What do you do if a deadline is simply
unchangeable?

Response: This is really a time allocation issue, as not all deadlines are inappropriate. The question implies that
there is not enough time to explore all the options.
Under time pressures we are inclined to turn to
cookie-cutter solutions, yet even under the most
aggressive deadlines, time should be set aside to
explore alternatives. For instance, a communication consultant was given a half-day to develop a
major communication strategy. The clients were
pressing him to "tell us what to do." He resisted
and instead spent 75 percent of the time exploring

and analyzing the situation. Once the team reached agreement on the nature of the situation, it only took about one hour to figure out what to do.[2]

Question: Are you saying organizations should forget about all long-range planning?

Response: Not necessarily. Long-range planning may be appropriate, but there is a limit to its utility. Inevitably, overly detailed plans will have to be changed, so planning for different contingencies or scenarios can be particularly helpful. This will make it easier to flexibly respond to the immediate situation.

Question: When I put together a report, my boss asks me to put the action steps on the front page. I don't think she even reads the rest of the report. Is this appropriate?

Response: In order to save time, many businesses have turned to this approach. It is a way to narrow down the choices and create certainty. Often this is unwise because it focuses discussion on "what to do" rather than "the possibilities of the situation." So you might try discussing the analysis and possibilities up front, accompanying this commentary with an explanation of why you chose this order.

Question: Why do some people continue to crave certainty even when it is clear that no one can really provide it?

Response: Ralph Stacy, the director of the Complexity and Management Center at the Business School of the University of Hertfordshire, may have put it best:

"The denial of uncertainty itself allows us to sustain the fantasy of someone up there being in control and, perhaps, of things turning out for the best if we simply do what we are told, and so it protects us for a while from anxiety."[3] The key point is that the "protection" is an illusion that lasts only for a short while.

"How Far Do You Go?" Issues

Question: Can I say "I don't know" too often?

Response: Embracing uncertainty doesn't mean you have to start a love affair with it.

Question: You have discussed the downside to certainty. What is the downside to uncertainty?

Response: You can be overwhelmed by the possibilities. You can also *appear* indecisive, bungling, and foolish. Like any philosophy, it can be purposely misunderstood. Embracing uncertainty is not a legitimate excuse for irresponsibility, complacency, and sloth.

Question: Do you think embracing uncertainty is desirable in all situations?

Response: No. Embracing uncertainty takes more mental energy than using cookie-cutter solutions. Since our mental energies are limited, you may have to be somewhat selective.

Question: Are you saying we should ignore the experts?

Response: No. But be cautious. In particular, be wary of those who seem overly sure of themselves.

Question: Are you legitimizing ignorance?

Response: It *is not* okay to be stupid. It *is* okay to admit you don't know.

Question: Aren't you really just advocating a "go-with-the-flow" attitude?

Response: Only in the sense that we want to discourage forcing solutions to problems before exploring legitimate alternatives.

Question: Are you saying that we shouldn't "look before we leap"?

Response: No. But you can't always see everything before you leap. Sometimes you have to take a few steps then look around and reassess the situation.

Ethical Issues

Question: I am a religious person, and I am absolutely certain about my faith. Is my faith incompatible with your philosophy?

Response: Consider one of the most treasured passages in the Bible (New Revised Standard Version):

> For we know only in part, and we prophesy only in part; but when the complete comes, the partial will come to an end. When I was a child, I spoke like a child, I thought like a child, I reasoned like a child; when I became an adult, I put an end to childish ways. For now we see in a mirror, dimly, but then we will see face to face. Now I know only in part; then I will know fully, even as I have been fully known. (*1 Corinthians 13: 9–13*)

Note the acceptance of the unknown as a natural part of the human condition.

Question: Don't some politicians use the "embrace uncertainty" philosophy to avoid responsibility for things they really should know?

Response: Sure. But we are not suggesting that they should use this philosophy to avoid responsibility. In fact, many politicians have perfected the art of "plausible deniability." This means that they make statements that have enough wiggle room that allows them to escape responsibility. Ignorance is not an excuse for irresponsibility.

Question: Do the "certainty merchants" know what they're doing?

Response: Some do. Most don't. They honestly believe in what they are doing. They unwittingly deceive themselves. Since they honestly believe in what they are doing, they are all the more persuasive. That's really scary.

Question: Are the "certainty merchants" unethical?

Response: Some are dishonest, and they know it. Those who don't know it, should know the limits of their knowledge. This represents not only their personal failure, but also a failure of the education and training they receive.

Question: Aren't there times when embracing uncertainty is unethical?

Response: Sure. A doctor who unwittingly gives a patient a drug that she is allergic to has an ethical dilemma. The doctor should have known but did not. We expect professionals to know certain things. Pleading ignorance is not always a valid excuse.

Tendency Issues

Question: I seem to tolerate some kinds of uncertainty better than others do. Is that natural?

Response: Perhaps. There are different types of uncertainty that people face in life. You might, for instance, be far more tolerant of uncertainty in your social life than in your work life. But we all can enhance our skills.

Question: Are there types of personalities that are more prone to certainty than others?

Response: Probably. People who are more intuitive tend to tolerate uncertainty more than others. However, psychologists are still debating the precise meaning of personality. One of the critical issues is whether our personalities are stable across situations. With that said, there are probably some people more naturally tolerant of the unknown than others. That does not mean they are incapable of using the exploring tools. Leaders should not use their personality type as an excuse to avoid self-development.

Question: Are there certain professions that are more likely to be comfortable with uncertainty?

Response: Our training and educational experiences tend to structure our sensibilities. Linear thinking tends to make us less tolerant of uncertainty. Consequently, there is a tendency for certain professionals such as engineers and accountants to be more comfortable with checklists and the other refining tools. Yet engineers are like anyone else; they can learn to effectively use the exploring tools, as well. We have found that those who work in nonprofit organizations tend to embrace less uncertainty than those who work in different types of organizations (see Appendix C).

Question: Are certain cultures more comfortable with uncertainty than others?

Response: Probably. Western culture tends to value certainty-making tools, while Eastern cultures tend to validate uncertainty. In fact, we in the process of studying this issue.

Question: Are males or females more tolerant of uncertainty?

Response: Our databank reveals that males tend to embrace uncertainty in the workplace more frequently than females (see Appendix C).

Question: Is there an age at which it is easier to embrace uncertainty?

Response: Children seem to be the most at ease with uncertainty. Their endless questions are driven more by a sense of curiosity than a need for structure. They are usually exploring. This childlike sense of wondering and wandering is what many adults need to recapture. However, our data bank reveals few discernable differences based on age.

Question: Are there times when we are particularly vulnerable to the illusion of certainty?

Response: There is a tendency to look for certainty under conditions of high anxiety or self-doubt.

Next-Step Issues

Question: What if I want to read more about this idea?

Response: We've included a reading list at the end of the book.

Question: Can I get any further help with "embracing uncertainty"?

Response: We've prepared some helpful exercises that can be found at the following website:
www.imetacomm.com/eu.

Question: Have you responded to all the major types of questions about uncertainty?

Response: No, we could not anticipate all of them. We *are* certain of that!

Notes

1. K. Kellermann and R. Reynolds, "When Ignorance Is Bliss: The Role of Motivation to Reduce Uncertainty in Uncertainty Reduction Theory," *Human Communication Theory* 17, no. 1 (1990): 5–75.

2. P. Clampitt and L. Berk, "Strategically Communicating Organisational Change," *Journal of Communication Management* 1, no. 1 (1996): 15–28.

3. R.D. Stacey, *Complexity and Creativity in Organizations* (San Francisco: Berrett-Koehler, 1996), p. 7.

Further Reading

W. Agor, *Intuition in Organizations: Leading and Managing Productively* (Newbury Park, CA: Sage, 1989).

P. L. Bernstein, *Against the Gods: The Remarkable Story of Risk* (New York: John Wiley, 1996).

J. Casti, *Complexification: Explaining a Paradoxical World Through the Science of Surprise* (New York: Harper Perennial, 1994).

P.G. Clampitt, R.J. DeKoch, and T. Cashman, "A Strategy for Communicating About Uncertainty," *The Academy of Management Executive* 14, no. 4 (2000): 41–57.

R. Feynman, *The Pleasure of Finding Things Out* (Cambridge, MA: Perseus Books, 1999).

S. Kelly and M.A. Allison, *The Complexity Advantage: How the Science of Complexity Can Help Your Business Achieve Peak Performance* (New York: McGraw-Hill, 1999).

R.D. Stacey, *Complexity and Creativity in Organizations* (San Francisco: Berrett-Koehler, 1996).

APPENDICES

DEVELOPED BY M. LEE WILLIAMS

Appendix A
THE WORKING CLIMATE SURVEY

You can take this survey online at www.imetacomm.com/eu, and it will be scored automatically. Otherwise, you can complete the survey below and score it using the procedures in Appendix B.

Objective

The purpose of this survey is to accurately describe your working climate. Please note:

- Your responses are confidential.
- This is *not* a test.
- There are no right or wrong answers.

Instructions

Below you will find a series of statements about your approach to various situations. Some items may sound similar, but they address slightly different issues. Please respond to all items. *Indicate your degree of agreement with each statement by placing the appropriate number on the line next to each item.* Please use the following scale:

1	2	3	4	5	6	7
Strongly Disagree	Moderately Disagree	Slightly Disagree	No Feeling	Slightly Agree	Moderately Agree	Strongly Agree

Section A: These Questions Concern Your Preferred Individual Style of Working

1. I'm comfortable making a decision on my gut instincts. _____
2. I actively look for signs that the situation is changing. _____
3. I need precise plans before starting a job. _____
4. When I start a project, I need to know exactly where I'll end up. _____
5. I'm comfortable using my intuition to make a decision. _____
6. I'm always on the lookout for new ideas to address problems. _____
7. I need to know the specific outcome before starting a task. _____
8. I'm quick to notice when circumstances change. _____
9. I'm willing to make a decision based on a hunch. _____
10. I easily spot changing trends. _____
11. I don't need a detailed plan when working on a project. _____
12. I'm skilled at making decisions when information is limited. _____
13. I need a definite sense of direction for a project. _____
14. I'm comfortable deciding on the spur-of-the-moment. _____
15. I'm comfortable with uncertainty. _____
16. I'm satisfied with my job. _____
17. I'm committed to my organization. _____
18. I'm satisfied with the communication in my organization. _____
19. I identify with my organization's values. _____
20. The longer I work in this organization, the more cynical I become. _____
21. I'm satisfied with the communication from my supervisor. _____
22. I'm a highly productive member of my organization. _____

1	2	3	4	5	6	7
Strongly Disagree	Moderately Disagree	Slightly Disagree	No Feeling	Slightly Agree	Moderately Agree	Strongly Agree

Section B: The Following Questions Concern Your Work Environment

23. My organization is always on the lookout for new ideas to address problems. _____

24. My organization flexibly responds to different situations. _____

25. In my organization, being unsure about something is a sign of weakness. _____

26. My organization easily spots changing trends. _____

27. My organization doesn't need a detailed plan when working on a project. _____

28. Even after my organization makes a decision, it will reevaluate the decision when the situation changes. _____

29. My organization needs to know the specific outcome before starting a project. _____

30. My organization doesn't encourage employees to discuss their doubts about a project. _____

31. When my organization starts a project, it needs to know exactly where the project will end up. _____

32. My organization actively looks for signs that the situation is changing. _____

33. My organization doesn't want employees to admit that they are unsure about something. _____

34. My organization wants precise plans before starting a job or project. _____

35. My organization discourages employees from talking about their misgivings. _____

36. Many employees in my organization are cynical. _____

37. My organization is concerned about employee satisfaction. _____

38. Many employees in my organization feel overwhelmed by the degree of change. _____

39. My organization is comfortable with uncertainty. _____

Appendix B
SCORING AND INTERPRETING
THE WORKING CLIMATE SURVEY

Scoring Section A—Personal Uncertainty (PU)

A "Strongly Agree" response to an item on the scale is scored "7" while a "Strongly Disagree" response is scored "1." However, since some of the items are positively worded and some are negatively worded, these scores must be converted to be meaningful. Begin by inserting your score for each corresponding item in the space provided. Use the following procedures to compute your personal uncertainty score. As an alternative, you can have your score computed automatically at www.imetacomm.com/eu.

Step 1: Personal Uncertainty Perceptual Score

Start with your score for item #2, add your score for item #6, add your score for item #8, and add your score for #10. Record the total of these 4 scores.

(#2) + (#6) + (#8) + (#10) = PU Perceptual Score

____ plus ____ plus ____ plus ____ = _____

Step 2: Personal Uncertainty Process Score

Start with your score for item #1, add your score for item #5, add your score for item #9, and add your score for item #14. Record the total of these 4 scores.

(#1) + (#5) + (#9) + (#14) = PU Process Score

____ plus ____ plus____ plus ____ = _____

Step 3: Personal Uncertainty Outcome Score

Start with a value of 24, subtract your score for item #4, subtract your score for item #7, add your score for item #11, and subtract your score for item #13. Record the total of these 5 scores.

24 – (#4) – (#7) + (#11) – (#13) = PU Outcome Score

_24_ minus ____ minus ____ plus ____ minus ____ = _____

Step 4: Overall Personal Uncertainty Score

Start with your PU Perceptual Score, add your PU Process Score, and add your PU Outcome Score. Record the total of these 3 scores.

Perceptual Score + Process Score + Outcome Score = **Overall PU Score**

_____ + _____ + _____ = ☐

Scoring Section B — Work Environment Uncertainty (WEU)

Step 1: Work Environment Uncertainty Perceptual Score

Start with your score for item #23, add your score for item #26, add your score for item #28, and add your score for item #32. Record the total of these 4 scores.

(#23) + (#26) + (#28) + (#32) = WEU Perceptual Score

_____ + _____ + _____ + _____ = _____

Step 2: Work Environment Uncertainty Expressed Score

Start with a value of 32, subtract your score for item #25, subtract your score for item #30, subtract your score for item #33, and subtract your score for item #35. Record the total of these 5 scores.

32 – (#25) – (#30) – (#33) – (#35) = WEU Expressed Score

__32__ minus _____ minus _____ minus _____ minus _____ = _____

Step 3: Work Environment Uncertainty Outcome Score

Start with a value of 24, add your score for item #27, subtract your score for item #29, subtract your score for item #31, and subtract your score for item #34. Record the total of these 5 scores.

24 + (#27) – (#29) – (#31) – (#34) = WEU Outcome Score

__24__ plus _____ minus _____ minus _____ minus _____ = _____

Step 4: Overall Work Environment Uncertainty Score

Start with your WEU Perceptual Score, add your WEU Expressed Score, and add your WEU Outcome Score. Record the total of these 3 scores.

Perceptual Score + Expressed Score + Outcome Score = **Overall WEU Score**

_____ plus _____ plus _____ = ☐

Note: Some survey items are not used in the computation of the scores above.

Interpreting Your Overall Scores

For the Overall Personal Uncertainty Score, the larger the value, the greater the tendency to embrace uncertainty. Your score can range from 12 (low) to 84 (high). Normative data ($n = 789$) indicate the median score for personal uncertainty is 57, the mean is 57.31, and the standard deviation is 8.11.

For the Overall Work Environment Uncertainty Score the larger the value, the greater you see the organization's tendency to embrace uncertainty. Scores can range from 12 (low) to 84 (high). Normative data ($n = 789$) indicate the median score for work environment uncertainty is 51, the mean is 51.75, and the standard deviation is 9.66.

Another way to look at your scores is to plot them on the grid in Figure B.1.

Step 1. Place a mark on the Y-axis that indicates your Overall Personal Uncertainty Score.

Step 2. Place a mark on the X-axis that indicates your Overall Work Environment Uncertainty Score.

Step 3. Find the intersection of the points.

By locating your scores on the grid in Figure B.2, you can determine which of the quadrants discussed in the introduction (Status Quo, Unsettling, Dynamic, Stifling) characterize your scores.

Figure B.1   **Plotting Your Score**

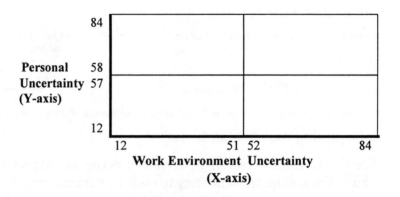

Figure B.2   **The Uncertainty Management Matrix**

	Stifling Climate 3	Dynamic Climate 4
	Status Quo Climate 1	Unsettling Climate 2

Employee's Approach to Uncertainty — *Embrace* (top) / *Avoid* (bottom)

Avoid   *Embrace*

Organization's Approach to Uncertainty

Appendix C
NORMATIVE DATA RESULTS

The initial development of scale items for *The Working Climate Survey* was conducted in 1999. After improving and replacing items on the scale, the completed version of *The Working Climate Survey* was administered to employees in a variety of types of organizations across the United States and Canada in 2000. A total of 789 individuals had completed the survey by October 2000. The results that follow are based on the norms produced from these 789 respondents. Table C.1 summarizes the characteristics of the database.

Based on their scores on *The Working Climate Survey*, respondents were placed in 1 of 4 climates: Status Quo Climate ($n = 224, 28\%$), Unsettling Climate ($n = 175, 22\%$), Stifling Climate ($n = 172, 22\%$), and Dynamic Climate ($n = 218, 28\%$). If an item on the survey was left blank, the mean score for that item was used to replace the missing value.

The Uncertainty Management Matrix Percentage Norms Table (see Table C.2) presents each of the four climates and the percentage of employees who agree with these survey items. Key demographics are also provided. An analysis of these climates indicates that:

- Proportionately more women are in the Unsettling and Status Quo Climates (both of which are climates where employees avoid uncertainty) than in the Dynamic and Stifling Climates (see Figure C.1).
- A larger proportion of top managers and managers are in the Dynamic Climate and Stifling Climate. These are

Table C.1

Database Characteristics

Gender	Males	36%
	Females	64%
Average age	39.4 yrs. (range: 16–74 yrs. old)	
Average job tenure	7 yrs. (range: 1 mo.–40 yrs.)	
Job positions	Top management	9%
	Management	40%
	Nonmanagement professional	27%
	Nonmanagement	19%
	Other	5%
Industries represented	Education, Government, Health Care, Retail, Hospitality, Sales/Marketing, Insurance, Financial, Media/Communications, Technology, Research/Publishing, Transportation, Manufacturing, Construction, Utility	
Countries represented	United States, Canada	

climates where employees embrace uncertainty (see Figure C.2).

· Proportionately, more employees who work for nonprofit organizations are in the Status Quo Climate than in other climates (see Figure C.3).

· Employees in the Dynamic and Unsettling Climates (both of which are climates where employees see their organization embracing uncertainty) express more satisfaction with their jobs, more commitment to their organizations, greater identification with their organizations, more satisfaction with organizational communication, more satisfaction with the communication with their supervisors, and less cynicism about organizational life (see Figure C.4).

· Employees in the Status Quo and Stifling Climates (both of which are climates where employees see their orga-

Table C.2

Uncertainty Management Matrix Percentage Norms Table

Embrace

	Stifling Climate	Dynamic Climate
	76% satisfied with job 77% committed to organization 64% identify with organization 36% satisfied with organization communication 52% satisfied with supervisor communication 59% cynical about organizational life 43% nonmanagerial 57% top management and managers 42% male, 58% female	90% satisfied with job 96% committed to organization 89% identify with organization 62% satisfied with organization communication 71% satisfied with supervisor communication 25% cynical about organizational life 43% nonmanagerial 57% top management and managers 46% male, 54% female

Employee's perspective

	Status Quo Climate	Unsettling Climate
	75% satisfied with job 81% committed to organization 64% identify with organization 44% satisfied with organization communication 43% satisfied with supervisor communication 45% cynical about organizational life 54% nonmanagerial 46% top management and managers 29% male, 71% female	90% satisfied with job 94% committed to organization 82% identify with organization 63% satisfied with organization communication 76% satisfied with supervisor communication 29% cynical about organizational life 54% nonmanagerial 46% top management and managers 27% male, 73% female

Avoid

Avoid   Embrace

Organization's perspective

nization avoiding uncertainty) express less satisfaction with their jobs, less commitment to their organizations, less identification with their organizations, less satisfaction with organizational communication, less satisfaction with the communication with their supervisors, and more cynicism about organizational life.

Overall, these results suggest the following order of desirability of organizational climates:

Most desirable	Dynamic climate
	Unsettling climate
	Stifling climate
Least desirable	Status quo climate

Figure C.1   **Climates by Gender**

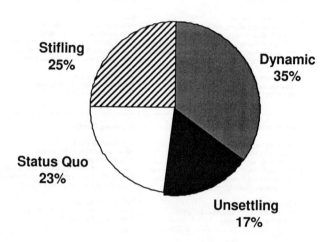

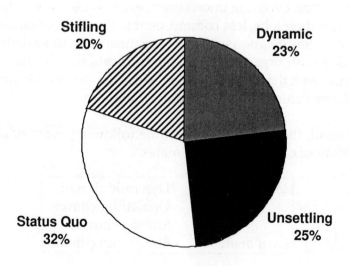

Figure C.2   **Climates by Job Classification**

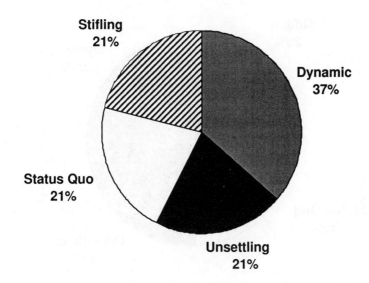

Top management

Stifling
21%

Dynamic
37%

Status Quo
21%

Unsettling
21%

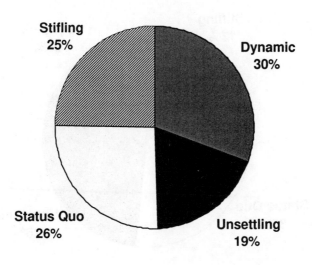

Management

Stifling
25%

Dynamic
30%

Status Quo
26%

Unsettling
19%

Figure C.2   **Climates by Job Classification** *(continued)*

Nonmanagement professional

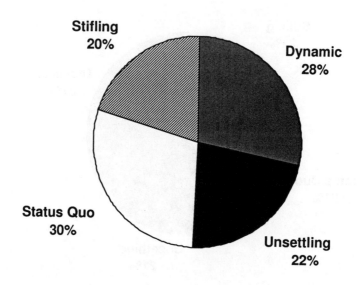

Stifling 20%

Dynamic 28%

Status Quo 30%

Unsettling 22%

Nonmanagement

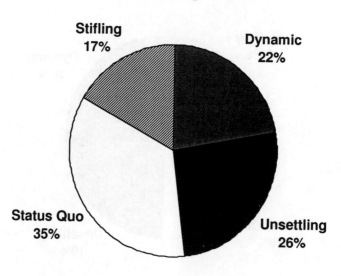

Stifling 17%

Dynamic 22%

Status Quo 35%

Unsettling 26%

Figure C.3 **Climates by Type of Organization**

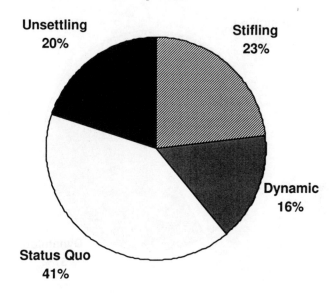

Nonprofit

Unsettling
20%

Stifling
23%

Dynamic
16%

Status Quo
41%

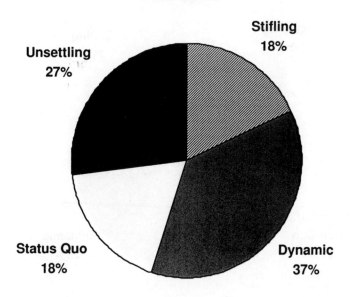

Financial

Stifling
18%

Unsettling
27%

Status Quo
18%

Dynamic
37%

Figure C.3   **Climates by Type of Organization** *(continued)*

Information/Technology

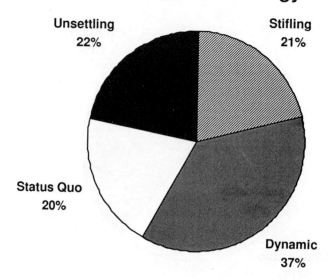

Service

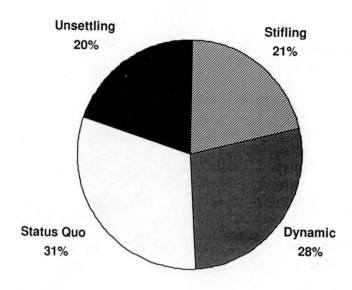

Figure C.3 **Climates by Type of Organization** *(continued)*

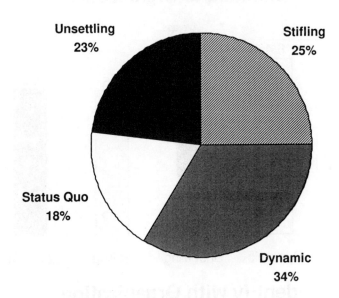

Industrial

Unsettling
23%

Stifling
25%

Status Quo
18%

Dynamic
34%

Figure C.4 **Relationship Between Climate and Outcome Variables**

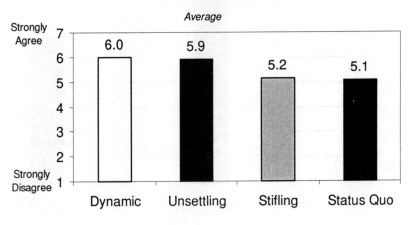

Satisfied with Job

Average

Strongly Agree 7

6.0   5.9   5.2   5.1

Strongly Disagree 1

Dynamic   Unsettling   Stifling   Status Quo

Figure C.4   **Relationship Between Climate and Outcome Variables**
(continued)

Committed to Organization

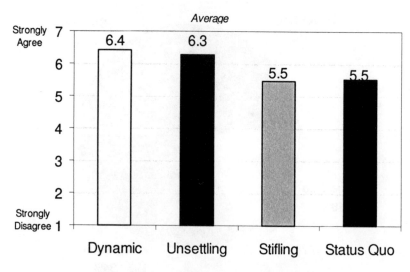

Identify with Organization

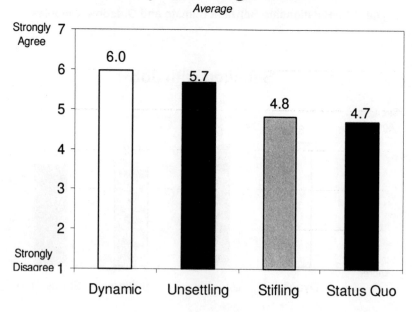

Figure C.4   **Relationship Between Climate and Outcome Variables**
(continued)

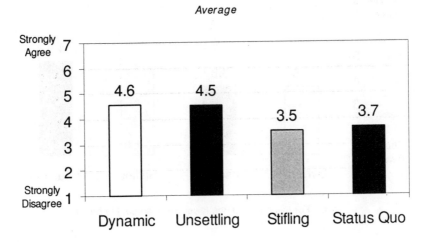

Satisfied with Organizational Communication

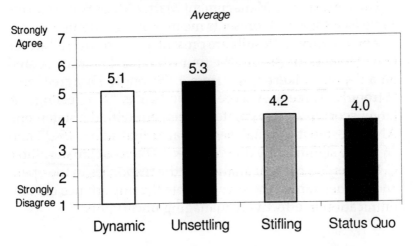

Satisfied with Supervisory Communication

Figure C.4   **Relationship Between Climate and Outcome Variables**
(continued)

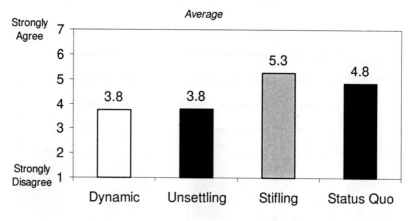

Cynical About Organizational Life*

Average

Note: For this question, the lower the average, the better.

The Uncertainty Management Matrix Mean Score Norms Table (see Table C.3) presents mean scores for items and factors on the survey. Results are presented for the overall scores (n = 789) and for each of the four climates. Items are scored on a 7–point Likert scale (from 1 "Strongly Disagree" to 7 "Strongly Agree"). A score of 4 indicates "No Feeling." A larger score indicates greater agreement with the statement. ANOVA statistical analyses revealed that items 15–22 and 36–39 are significantly different ($p < .01$) across climates. Table C.4 presents a content analysis of the responses to the open-ended question on the survey. Note the importance of communication in effectively managing uncertainty.

Table C.3

Uncertainty Management Matrix Mean Score Norms Table

The *Working Climate Survey* Item/Factor*	Overall (n = 789)	Status Quo Climate (n = 224)	Unsettling Climate (n = 175)	Stifling Climate (n = 172)	Dynamic Climate (n = 218)
15. I'm comfortable with uncertainty.	3.64	2.96	3.13	4.09	4.40
16. I'm satisfied with my job.	5.53	5.08	5.91	5.16	5.98
17. I'm committed to my organization.	5.93	5.54	6.27	5.48	6.42
18. I'm satisfied with the communication in my organization.	4.07	3.65	4.53	3.51	4.57
19. I identify with my organization's values.	5.29	4.70	5.67	4.81	5.97
20. The longer I work in this organization, the more cynical I become.	3.59	4.07	3.06	4.39	2.89
21. I'm satisfied with the communication from my supervisor.	4.61	3.95	5.34	4.15	5.06
22. I'm a highly productive member of my organization.	6.17	6.02	6.04	6.16	6.43
36. Many employees in my organization are cynical.	4.39	4.83	3.78	5.25	3.75
37. My organization is concerned about employee satisfaction.	4.69	3.87	5.57	3.90	5.46
38. Many employees in my organization feel overwhelmed by the degree of change.	4.37	4.54	4.14	4.79	4.03
39. My organization is comfortable with uncertainty.	3.70	3.27	3.97	3.44	4.14
41. Age	39.35 yrs	40.11 yrs	38.22 yrs	40.39 yrs	38.64 yrs
42. Job Tenure	7.00 yrs	6.44 yrs	6.13 yrs	8.68 yrs	6.71 yrs
Personal Uncertainty (12 items)	57.31	50.66	51.26	63.48	64.11
Perceptual	21.84	20.17	20.70	23.06	23.51
Process	20.27	18.41	17.46	22.84	22.41
Outcome	15.20	12.08	13.10	17.58	18.19

(continued)

Table C.3 (continued)

The Working Climate Survey Item/Factor*	Overall (n = 789)	Status Quo Climate (n = 224)	Unsettling Climate (n = 175)	Stifling Climate (n = 172)	Dynamic Climate (n = 218)
Work Uncertainty (12 items)	51.75	44.11	58.05	43.94	60.72
Perceptual	18.73	16.21	20.80	16.60	21.35
Expressed	18.61	15.17	21.99	14.53	22.66
Work Outcome	14.41	12.74	15.25	12.81	16.72

Notes: ANOVAs for items 15–22 and 36–39 confirmed significant differences ($p < .01$) across climates.

*Items were scored on a 7-point Likert scale (from 1 "Strongly Disagree" to 7 "Strongly Agree"). A score of 4 indicated "No Feeling." A larger score indicates greater agreement with the statement.

Table C.4

Analysis of Responses to Open-Ended Question: "How Could Your Organization Make You More Comfortable Managing Uncertainty in the Workplace?"

Rank	Percentage of respondents	Category	Sample comments
1	69	Better communication	"Better and more timely management to employee communication."
			"Communicate the 'not so good' with the great."
			"Explain the 'unknowns' as best they can with risk assessments. Keep everyone aware of these issues."
			"Listen!"
			"Explain changes before they appear in the newspaper."
2	43	More information	"Staying informed on trends and actively seek to project impact of those trends."
			"Providing more information about changes to be made."
			"Provide more information."
3	18	Improved decision making	"They could encourage employee decisions instead of second guessing."
			"Less micromanagement."
			"Freedom to deviate from policy and procedure when exceptions arise."
			"Give us the freedom to make the decisions we were hired to make and provide support for the decisions made."
4	5	Other	"Start out with a more definitive plan and stay consistent."
			"Stop changing the rules daily."
			"Control amount of information coming in and forced on employees."

Note: The percentages do not total 100 percent because many respondents made comments that fell into more than one category.

Appendix D
THE HISTORY OF THE INSTRUMENT

The development of *The Work Climate Survey* spanned several years and involved three phases:

Phase One

In Phase One, the theoretical rationale for the survey was developed, and more than 90 items were used to measure how employees managed uncertainty, as well as how they perceived their organization managing uncertainty. Organizational liaisons in various states distributed the survey to over 200 employees working in a wide variety of organizations. Results were factor-analyzed, and standard statistical procedures used in scale development were employed. To refine the survey, items were reworded, deleted, or replaced.

Phase Two

In this phase, the survey was administered to another cross-section of employees ($n = 239$). Analysis of this version of the instrument produced 12 items designed to measure how employees managed uncertainty. These items were grouped into three factors:

· Perceptual Uncertainty
· Process Uncertainty

· Outcome Uncertainty*

Another 11 items measured employees' perceptions of how their organization managed uncertainty, which also clustered into three factors:

· Perceptual Uncertainty
· Expressed Uncertainty
· Outcome Uncertainty*

Using standard psychometric techniques, the validity and reliability of the uncertainty management instruments were also confirmed in this analysis. Results indicated the following:

· An employee who does not embrace uncertainty is also intolerant of ambiguous situations ($r = -.40, p < .001$).
· Employees who embrace uncertainty (as measured on the twelve-item scale) also tended to agree with a single item measuring comfort with uncertainty (i.e., I'm comfortable with uncertainty) ($r = .39, p < .001$). However, employee uncertainty was not significantly correlated with gender ($r = -.07$), age ($r = -.05$), or tenure in the organization ($r = .05$).
· Individual uncertainty was significantly correlated with managerial level ($r = -.23, p < .001$), thus indicating employees in nonmanagerial positions do not embrace uncertainty as much as employees in managerial positions.
· Personal uncertainty was not correlated with social de-

---

*We based the model discussed in Chapter 7 on these factors. The "Perceptual Uncertainty" factors equate to the "Cultivating Awareness" component of the model. We combined the "Personal Process Uncertainty" and "Work Environment Expressed Uncertainty" factors into the "Processing Uncertainty" component of the model. The "Outcome Uncertainty" factors equate to the "Catalyzing Action" component of the model.

sirability ($r = .05$), nor was it correlated with a single item measure of job satisfaction (i.e., I'm satisfied with my job) ($r = .10$) or commitment (i.e., I'm committed to my organization) ($r = .12$).

How employees perceived their organization managing uncertainty was also correlated with a variety of other scales. The findings revealed that:

· The organization's approach to uncertainty was not correlated with intolerance of ambiguity ($r = -.02$), thus indicating employees' personal tolerance of ambiguity was not related to how they perceived their organization managing uncertainty.
· Organizational management of uncertainty was not correlated with the individual's comfort with uncertainty ($r = -.02$), gender ($r = -.02$), age ($r = .01$), tenure in the organization ($r = .07$), or managerial level ($r = -.07$).
· The organizational uncertainty dimension was significantly correlated with job satisfaction ($r = .49, p < .001$), commitment ($r = .43, p < .001$), and the organization's concern with employee satisfaction (i.e., My organization is concerned with employee satisfaction) ($r = .64, p < .001$).
· Organizational uncertainty was minimally correlated with social desirability ($r = .15, p < .02$), explaining only 2 percent of the variance.
· The organizational uncertainty measure was not significantly correlated with the employee uncertainty measure ($r = .06$).

Phase Three

There were two primary objectives for this phase:

1. Fine-tune the instrument by testing several revised items to create a 12–item scale for both the employee uncer-

tainty and organizational uncertainty dimensions.

2. Build the database. An additional sample of respondents was asked to fill out the survey in an effort to increase the employee database.

Both objectives were successfully completed. Using organizational liaisons, responses from 789 employees across the United States and Canada were analyzed. Organizations represented in this sample included manufacturing, high tech, health care, financial services, government, and transportation.

This "final" version of the instrument (see Appendix A) is practical and easy to administer, as well as easy to tabulate and interpret (see Appendix B). The employee uncertainty (i.e., personal uncertainty) dimension has 12 items and an overall Cronbach's alpha reliability of .61. The three 4–item factors are:

1. Personal Perceptual Uncertainty—the employee's willingness to actively look at different perspectives, new ideas, or signs the situation is changing (alpha = .73).
2. Personal Process Uncertainty—the employee's comfort in making a decision based on an intuition or hunch (alpha = .78).
3. Personal Outcome Uncertainty—the employee's willingness to work without detailed plans and specific outcomes in mind (alpha = .79).

The organizational uncertainty (i.e., work environment uncertainty) dimension has 12 items and an overall Cronbach's alpha reliability of .70. The three 4–item factors are:

1. Work Environment Perceptual Uncertainty—the organization's willingness to actively look at different perspectives, new ideas, or signs the situation is changing (alpha = .75).
2. Work Environment Expressed Uncertainty—the

organization's willingness to encourage employees to express their doubts, misgivings, and hunches (alpha = .78).

3. Work Environment Outcome Uncertainty—the organization's willingness to work without detailed plans and specific outcomes in mind (alpha = .76).

These data were used to create the Uncertainty Management Matrix (see Appendix C). The matrix joins the individual employee's tolerance for uncertainty (as measured by the personal uncertainty scale) and the organization's desire to embrace uncertainty (as measured by the work environment uncertainty scale). The four climates produced from combining these two dimensions are:

1. Status Quo Climate—employees and the organization both avoid uncertainty. Employees want few surprises and they rarely get them.

2. Unsettling Climate—employees desire certainty while the organization is perceived as embracing too much uncertainty. Thus employees become unsettled and perhaps overwhelmed by the chaotic work environment.

3. Stifling Climate—employees embrace uncertainty but they perceive the organization avoiding it.

4. Dynamic Climate—both employees and the organization embrace uncertainty. Consequently, the climate is dynamic, energetic, and ever-changing.

For more details about the development process, consult "Other Publications" at www.imetacomm.com.

ABOUT THE AUTHORS

Phillip G. Clampitt received his Ph.D. in organizational communication from the University of Kansas. He is a full professor at the University of Wisconsin—Green Bay in the Information Sciences Program. He has published in various journals, including *The Academy of Management Executive, Journal of Communication Management, Journal of Business Communication, Management Communication Quarterly, Journal of Broadcasting,* and *Communication World.* He also is on the editorial board of numerous professional journals. His most recent book, *Communicating for Managerial Effectiveness* (2nd edition), is based on the research from past communication assessments. Professor Clampitt is also the founder of *Meta*Comm, a consulting firm that enables organizations to take their communication practices to a "higher plane" (see www.imetacomm.com). He has worked with numerous organizations over the past fifteen years.

Robert J. DeKoch received his B.A. from Lawrence University (Appleton, Wisconsin) and his M.B.A. from the University of Wisconsin. He has held numerous technical, manufacturing, and general management positions in a variety of industrial and service businesses. He is currently the Chief Operating Officer with a major U.S. consulting and construction company, The Boldt Company. Throughout his career, Mr. DeKoch has focused on developing work environments for high involvement and continuous learning. He has instituted progressive communication processes in the workplace to promote understanding, focus, and alignment. He strives to build work relationships that foster innovative thinking, recognition of achievement, and genuine teamwork.

M. Lee Williams received his Ph.D. from the University of Oklahoma. He is a professor in the Department of Speech Communication at Southwest Texas State University, where he has received the Presidential Award for Excellence in Teaching. His work has been published in various journals, including *Human Communication Research, Communication Monographs, Journal of Applied Communication Research, Communication Research Reports,* and *Journal of Leadership Studies.* He has conducted numerous communication audits and employee feedback surveys in organizations, and he serves as a consultant in communicating organizational change.

INDEX